Overnight wealth:

Quick Ways to Start Making Money by Tomorrow”

Daniel David

Dedication

To God
For the wisdom, strength, and grace to keep moving forward, even when the path is unclear. Every blessing, idea, and opportunity comes from You.

And to all the hustlers out there—
The dreamers, the doers, the ones who refuse to wait for perfect timing. This is for those who wake up hungry and go to bed tired, chasing something greater every single day.

Keep grinding. Keep believing. Your time is closer than you think.

First Edition

Table of Contents

Introduction

Why Hustle Overnight?

In a world where opportunities to make money are abundant, the real challenge lies in timing. Whether it's a sudden bill, an unexpected opportunity, or a desire to level up your finances, the need for quick cash can show up at any moment. This is where hustling overnight comes in. It's about taking action today, so that you're seeing results by tomorrow.

Overnight hustles aren't about striking it rich in a single day. They're about smart, simple strategies that leverage your time, skills, and resources to generate cash fast. You don't need an advanced degree or piles of capital. You just need a plan, a little creativity, and the willingness to get started.

These hustles are realistic, practical, and, most importantly, accessible. The goal is to help you earn money quickly and efficiently, whether you have an hour to spare or a whole weekend ahead. Anyone, anywhere, can jump in—no waiting for "the right time." If you need cash now, the time is now.

The Mindset for Quick Cash

The most important thing to get right when hustling overnight is your mindset. Making money quickly isn't about luck—it's about having the right attitude and being prepared to take immediate action.

1. Action Over Perfection: Don't wait until you know everything before getting started. The perfect plan is less important than the first step. The more you do, the more you'll learn and adjust.

2. Adaptability: Flexibility is key. Whether you're offering a service or selling a product, things won't always go according to plan. Be ready to pivot or adapt quickly to what works and what doesn't.

3. Focus: Multi-tasking might sound productive, but when hustling for quick cash, focus is your friend. Work on one hustle at a time and give it your full attention. You'll see results faster.

4. Resilience: Hustling isn't always smooth sailing. Some ideas won't work right away—and that's okay. Use failure as a stepping stone to improve. Keep pushing forward, and you'll find the success you're looking for.

Ground Rules: Legal, Ethical, and Realistic

Before jumping into any hustle, there are a few essential ground rules you need to follow. These will ensure your hustle is sustainable, reputable, and ultimately successful.

1. Stay Legal: Quick cash doesn't have to mean cutting corners. Always ensure that your hustle follows the laws and regulations that apply to your location and the type of work you're doing. Whether it's taxes, permits, or copyright issues, staying legal is non-negotiable.

2. Be Ethical: Hustling should be about providing value, not exploiting others. Whether you're freelancing, selling products, or offering a service, your reputation is everything. Be transparent, fair, and deliver on your promises. This will build trust and bring you repeat customers.

3. Be Realistic: While it's exciting to think about making tons of money fast, it's crucial to have realistic expectations. Some hustles may yield quick returns, while others may take a bit more time to grow. Know your limits in terms of time, energy, and skill. Start small and build momentum from there.

With the right mindset and a strong foundation of legal, ethical, and realistic principles, you're now ready to explore the many ways you can start making money today. Let's get hustling.

Part I: Digital Hustles You Can Start Tonight

1.

Freelancing Fast: Getting Your First Gig on Fiverr or Upwork

In today's digital world, your skills are currency—and freelancing is one of the fastest ways to turn those skills into cash. Whether you're a writer, designer, video editor, translator, voice-over artist, or even just someone with a good grasp of the English language, there's a market out there for you. Platforms like Fiverr and Upwork have created entire ecosystems where clients are actively looking to hire people for small, quick-turnaround jobs—many of which pay within days. The beauty of freelancing is that you don't need a resume full of awards or a flashy portfolio to get started. What you do need is a clear value offer, the courage to put yourself out there, and the commitment to deliver your best—fast.

The Power of Positioning Yourself

The first step to landing a freelance gig isn't finding the right client—it's presenting yourself as the right freelancer. Imagine walking into a marketplace with hundreds of people selling apples. If yours isn't shinier, cheaper, more flavorful, or more creatively packaged, it's easy to get lost in the noise. On Fiverr and Upwork, this starts with your profile and gig listings. This is your digital storefront, and it needs to be tight. Take your time to write a professional but friendly bio. Don't just list your skills—talk about the value you offer. Instead of saying, "I write blog posts," say, "I help businesses grow their audience with SEO-friendly, engaging blog content that speaks directly to their target readers." That small shift in language turns you from a generalist into a problem-solver—and that's what clients are really buying.

Upload a photo of yourself that looks approachable and professional. If you're camera-shy, consider using a logo or graphic, but remember—people hire people. A face helps build trust. Add a video introduction if the platform allows it. You don't have to be a great speaker—just be real. Even a 30-second video can dramatically increase your chances of getting hired because it adds personality and shows initiative. These little touches show potential clients that you're not only skilled but also serious.

What to Offer When You're Just Starting Out

One of the biggest myths that stops people from freelancing is the idea that they need to be an expert. The truth? You don't. You just need to be one step ahead of the client you're helping. There are thousands of people every day looking for basic tasks: proofreading, transcribing audio, summarizing documents, resizing images, turning blog posts into social media quotes, or even organizing data into spreadsheets. These aren't glamorous jobs, but they pay—and most importantly, they help you build momentum.

Start by identifying 1–3 simple services you can confidently deliver in 24–48 hours. Fiverr is perfect for this. Create very specific gigs, like "I will write a 500-word blog post about health and fitness" or "I will edit your resume in 24 hours." On Upwork, you'll need to submit proposals for job postings, which means writing a short, compelling message that explains how you can help and why you're the right person. Again, keep the focus on their problem and your solution, not just your experience.

If you're still unsure what to offer, look around. Spend an hour browsing Fiverr and Upwork, not to get intimidated—but to get inspired. Search terms like "beginner," "new freelancer," "simple jobs," or even filter for gigs that require no experience. See what others are doing, and more importantly, what's getting ordered.

The Emotional Side of Your First Gig

There's something deeply nerve-wracking about putting yourself out there for the first time. Hitting "publish" on your first Fiverr gig or submitting your first Upwork proposal feels like shouting into a void. Will anyone hear you? Will anyone choose you? That fear is real. But here's the truth: every successful freelancer started in that exact same spot. No reviews. No ratings. No clients. Just hope, effort, and a little bit of courage.

Your first client may not pay much. It might be $5, $10, or $20. But that first job is more than a transaction—it's proof that you can do this. It's the start of your freelancing story. And once you complete one job and earn a good review, the snowball starts rolling. Your confidence builds. Your profile gains credibility. You stop feeling like an imposter and start feeling like a professional.

There's also joy in that first payment—no matter how small. When money lands in your PayPal or Upwork account for work you did independently, it hits differently. It's empowering. It's a taste of freedom. It reminds you that you don't have to wait for someone to give you permission to earn—you already have everything you need.

Speed vs. Quality: Finding the Balance

When hustling overnight, speed matters—but quality is what gets you repeat business. Clients will remember if you delivered fast, but they'll hire you again if you delivered well. That's where real income starts—not just from new clients, but from people who come back again and again because you made their life easier.

One strategy is to under-promise and over-deliver. If you say you'll deliver in 48 hours and you finish it in 24, you look efficient. If you say you'll provide three headlines and you give them five, you look generous. These little things cost you almost nothing but create massive goodwill. They also lead to five-star reviews—which are gold on platforms like Fiverr and Upwork.

Don't be afraid to say no to jobs that feel off. When you're just starting out, it's tempting to accept anything, but trust your gut. If something feels sketchy, unclear, or way outside your ability, it's okay to pass. There are thousands of other clients looking for someone just like you.

Getting Paid and Building Momentum

One of the great benefits of using platforms like Fiverr and Upwork is that they handle payment processing, so you don't need to chase clients down. Fiverr pays out 14 days after job completion, and Upwork has a 5-day security window after client approval. It's not instant, but it's reliable, and over time, you can create a system where you're getting paid consistently each week.

As you complete more jobs, raise your rates gradually. Don't be afraid to value your time. Start low if needed, but don't stay there. Clients will often judge your quality by your pricing, so raising your rates not only increases income—it increases perceived value.

Eventually, freelancing can become more than a side hustle. Many people begin by earning $20–$100 a day and scale that into a full-time income. But the key is starting. Not tomorrow. Tonight.

2.

Selling Digital Products or Art Online

There is something deeply satisfying about creating something once and being paid for it over and over again. That's the beauty of digital products. In a world where physical inventory comes with risks—shipping delays, overhead costs, and customer complaints—digital goods allow for passive income, low overhead, and unlimited scalability. For creatives, makers, or even people with just an idea and a little bit of patience, this hustle is one of the most powerful paths to financial independence—and you can start it tonight.

Understanding the Digital Product Hustle

Let's break this down simply: digital products are files—things you can download. They don't exist physically. They don't get lost in the mail. They don't have to be restocked. They live on your laptop, your iPad, or your imagination—and they're sold on platforms like Etsy, Gumroad, Payhip, or even your own website. These products could be ebooks, printables, coloring pages, art prints, music, stock photos, Lightroom presets, workout plans, spreadsheets, templates, or anything else someone can download and use.

And here's the magic: you only have to create them once. After that, you sell them over and over again with almost no extra work. That's what makes this hustle ideal for overnight starters—it rewards creativity, patience, and smart marketing over brute force labor. You may not make your first dollar tonight, but you can absolutely launch tonight—and that's the first step to a product that can generate income while you sleep.

Start with What You Have—Not What You Wish You Had

Too many people get stuck at the starting line because they think they need to be an expert, or that their product needs to be perfect. That's not true. What you need is to identify what you already know and package it in a way that solves a problem or inspires someone. For example, if you've ever planned a wedding, managed your monthly budget, journaled your way through a breakup, or organized your schedule with a digital calendar—you already have something valuable to share. That spreadsheet you made to stay on top of your bills? Someone would pay $4.99 for that. The playlist covers or wallpapers you doodled on your iPad? Someone is looking for that exact vibe right now.

Selling digital art or products isn't about being the best artist, designer, or thinker. It's about being relatable. It's about identifying a problem or a desire and offering something that scratches that itch. You don't need to create something groundbreaking—you just need to create something helpful, beautiful, or fun.

Choosing a Platform: Where Should You Sell?

Picking a platform can feel overwhelming, but don't overthink it. If you're creating aesthetic printables, templates, or art, Etsy is a fantastic place to start because it already has built-in traffic. People come to Etsy ready to buy. If your product is a bit more niche—like a personal finance tracker, self-help guide, or something more DIY or indie—then Gumroad or Payhip may be a better fit. These platforms are free or low-cost and allow you to set up a store in minutes, no coding or tech background required.

If you're more technically inclined or want full control, you can build a storefront on your own website using tools like Shopify, WordPress with WooCommerce, or Sellfy. But this route requires more setup and maintenance, so for overnight hustling, it's often better to start with Etsy or Gumroad. The goal is to get your first product live—not build an empire overnight.

Creating Your First Product: Keep It Simple

Here's the truth: the simpler your first product, the more likely you'll finish it and publish it. Don't try to create a 200-page ebook or an elaborate Notion system right away. Start with one thing. A single printable journal. A 7-day workout plan. A three-template resume kit. The key is to create something that offers value without overwhelming you.

If you're creating visual products like art prints, social media templates, or planner pages, use Canva, Procreate, or Adobe Express. Canva, especially, is free and incredibly powerful. You can use it to design digital planners, resume templates, business card designs, or even social media content packs that people can download and customize.

If you're creating more written-based products, like guides or trackers, use Google Docs, Microsoft Word, or Notion. Format your content clearly, save it as a PDF, and boom—you've got a sellable product.

Don't get hung up on perfection. The product you launch tonight will never be your best work—but it might be your most important, because it's the one that gets you in the game.

Branding and Presentation: Why First Impressions Matter

No matter how good your digital product is, people won't buy it if it doesn't look good. That doesn't mean you need to spend hours obsessing over a logo or theme, but you do need to pay attention to how your product is presented. Clear mockups, compelling descriptions, and cohesive colors can make a $5 product look like a $50 one.

Canva is your best friend here, again. Use it to create mockups—images that show your product in use. For example, if you're selling a digital planner, show what it looks like on an iPad. If you're selling wall art, show it in a frame on a living room wall. This isn't deceptive—it's emotional marketing. People don't buy files. They buy possibilities. They buy feelings. Help them imagine what your product will do for them.

When writing your product description, think like a customer. What problem does this solve? What transformation will they get? Keep your tone warm, clear, and helpful. This isn't a sales pitch—it's a conversation.

Pricing Your Product: Don't Sell Yourself Short

Pricing is a common sticking point. Many new sellers drastically undervalue their work, thinking that cheap prices will bring in more customers. But in the digital world, lower prices don't always mean more sales—they often mean less perceived value. That $3 worksheet might sell better at $9 if it looks high-quality and solves a specific problem.

Look at competitors. Search for similar products and see what they charge. Then ask yourself: what would you pay for your product if you were the customer? Remember, digital products have zero reproduction cost. You create it once, and every sale after that is profit. So don't be afraid to charge fairly. You can always adjust your pricing as you grow and collect reviews.

Driving Traffic: How to Get Your First Sale

Once your product is live, you might feel a moment of quiet panic. "Okay, it's out there... now what?" This is where the hustle begins. Because while passive income is real, it starts with active effort. No one can buy your product if they don't know it exists. So let's talk about getting those first eyeballs.

Use what you already have. Post on your Instagram, TikTok, or Facebook—even if your followers are mostly friends and family. Be genuine. Share the story behind the product. "I made this because I needed it, and I thought someone else might too." That authenticity matters. People want to support real people.

Join Facebook groups or Reddit communities related to your product's niche. Don't spam—contribute value first. Answer questions. Share helpful tips. Then gently introduce your product where it fits. One thoughtful post in a group of 10,000 can lead to your first 5–10 sales.

If you have time, consider posting a short demo video on TikTok or Instagram Reels. Showing how your product works or how it helps others is a powerful way to grab attention. You don't need to be an influencer. You just need to show up.

The Emotional Journey of Selling Something You Made

There is a vulnerable, raw kind of pride that comes with creating something from scratch and putting it into the world. It's thrilling, but also terrifying. You'll refresh your inbox a hundred times. You'll check your sales stats obsessively. You'll feel a strange cocktail of hope, doubt, and excitement. And when that first notification pops up—You've made a sale—something changes in you.

That tiny moment confirms that your ideas are worth something. That your creativity has value. That you don't have to wait for someone to hire you, promote you, or choose you. You've chosen yourself. And once that happens, you're no longer just a dreamer. You're a creator. An entrepreneur. A hustler.

3.

Affiliate Marketing with Zero Investment

There is a hidden army of people online who make money without ever creating a product, without holding inventory, without dealing with customers, and without ever handling returns or shipping. They aren't scammers or spammers—they're affiliate marketers. And the most surprising part? Many of them started with absolutely nothing but a phone, an internet connection, and the desire to hustle. Affiliate marketing is the art—and increasingly, the science—of earning money by recommending things people already want to buy. If you've ever told a friend about a product and they went and bought it, you've done the work of an affiliate marketer—you just didn't get paid for it. This chapter is going to change that.

Affiliate marketing sounds complicated at first, but it's one of the fastest, lowest-risk ways to begin earning online. You don't need your own website (though it helps), you don't need money for ads, and you don't need to be a salesperson. You just need to understand the core principle: when someone buys a product through your unique referral link, you earn a commission. And in many cases, that commission can come from things people already plan to buy. You're not interrupting people—you're helping them make better choices.

The Power of Recommendations in a Digital World

Let's be honest: we live in a world of too many choices. Whether it's tech gadgets, books, beauty products, tools, or courses, people are overwhelmed. That's where affiliate marketing becomes powerful—because when someone trusts your opinion and you guide them to something that makes their life easier, you're not just making a sale. You're solving a problem. And the internet rewards that. Whether through blogs, TikTok, YouTube,

Instagram, or even Facebook groups, authentic recommendations have become a currency of trust. And trust, more than anything, converts into income.

This is why affiliate marketing doesn't require you to be famous, have a huge following, or even be an expert. What it does require is clarity, consistency, and honesty. If you can share why a certain book helped you, or why you chose one budget laptop over another, or how a specific planner helped you stay on top of your goals, people will listen. And when they do, and they buy through your link, you get paid. That's the kind of win-win this hustle thrives on.

How It Works: A Simple Breakdown

Here's the simplest way to understand affiliate marketing: you sign up for an affiliate program, you get a special link to a product or service, and you share that link with others. When someone clicks your link and buys, you earn a commission, which can range from a few percent to as high as 50% or more, depending on the product. Sometimes it's a one-time payment, sometimes it's recurring (like for subscriptions).

There are hundreds of affiliate programs, but some of the most popular include:

- Amazon Associates – You can link to almost any product on Amazon.
- ShareASale, Impact, CJ Affiliate, and Rakuten – These are affiliate networks with thousands of companies.
- Individual programs – Many services (like Canva, ConvertKit, Bluehost, Skillshare) offer their own referral programs.
- Signing up is usually free and takes just minutes. And once you're approved, you can begin promoting products immediately.

Start Tonight: What Can You Recommend?

The beauty of this hustle is that you don't need to start from scratch. You already use things every day that others might want too. Think about what you genuinely love or rely on. What products make your life easier, more enjoyable, or more productive? That journal app you use? That wireless keyboard that changed your workflow? That budget hair product that outperforms salon brands? That beginner-friendly camera you used to start your content journey? Those are all affiliate opportunities.

Start with what you know. Make a list of:

- The products you use daily
- Apps or tools that saved you time
- Courses or ebooks that taught you something valuable
- Equipment or software you recommend to friends

Chances are, at least a few of them have affiliate programs. And if they do, you can start recommending them as early as tonight.

Where to Share Your Affiliate Links

Once you've picked a few products and signed up for their programs, the next step is getting people to see your links. This is where distribution becomes the heart of the hustle. And thankfully, there are more ways than ever to share without needing a blog or thousands of followers.

1. Social Media – If you use TikTok, Instagram, or Facebook, you already have an audience. You don't need to spam links. Instead, create posts that tell stories. "This $25 planner changed how I manage my week. Here's why." That's more powerful than a sales pitch. Add your link in your bio or in the comments.

2. TikTok & Reels – One viral video can generate affiliate income for weeks. Make short, honest videos showing how you use a product. "Top 3 Amazon finds for my small apartment" or "What I used to build my side hustle setup under $100." Be authentic. Let your excitement show. People respond to genuine energy.

3. Pinterest – Surprisingly, Pinterest is still a goldmine for affiliate marketers. You can create pins that link directly to products or blog posts with affiliate links. Tools like Canva make pin creation simple. And since Pinterest is a search engine, your content lasts longer than on Instagram or TikTok.

4. YouTube – If you're comfortable on camera, product reviews, unboxings, and tutorials are incredibly powerful. Even a small channel with 100 views can earn income if the product is relevant and the content is trustworthy. Always put your links in the description.

5. Email or DMs – This is underrated. If a friend asks for a product recommendation, send them your affiliate link. Don't be pushy—just be helpful. "Hey, here's the mic I mentioned! Full transparency: it's an affiliate link, but I really love it."

6. Quora and Reddit – If done respectfully, answering questions on platforms like Quora or Reddit can drive targeted traffic. Focus on giving real value. Help people solve problems. Then, only when appropriate, include your affiliate link or a link to a blog/video that includes it.

Your First Commission: The Emotional Rush

There's a special thrill to earning your first affiliate commission. It might only be $0.89 from a random Amazon sale, or $5 from a course someone clicked on through your link. But it will feel like a million dollars. Why? Because it confirms that you made money without working a job, without trading time for money, without selling your own product. You got paid for sharing something helpful. And in that moment, you realize: this is real. And scalable. And only the beginning.

That first commission is the proof you need to push harder. To keep creating. To trust the process.

Avoiding Pitfalls and Keeping It Ethical

Affiliate marketing gets a bad reputation because some people abuse it. They spam links. They promote things they've never used. They pressure people into buying. Don't be that person. Not only is it unethical—it doesn't work long-term.

Instead, build trust and consistency. Disclose when you're using affiliate links. Be honest about your experiences. Focus on helping, not selling. If a product has a downside, mention it. People respect transparency, and that builds loyalty. And when people trust you, they don't just buy once—they come back again and again.

Also, don't rely on just one product or platform. Diversify. Promote a few different products across a few channels. That way, if one link stops performing or a platform changes its algorithm, you're still in the game.

Scaling the Hustle: Turning Recommendations into Residual Income

Once you start making small commissions, it's time to think bigger. Could you build a simple blog where you review or compare products? Could you launch a newsletter sharing monthly product recommendations? Could you partner with other creators or offer affiliate bonuses for people who buy through your link? These are ways to turn a simple hustle into a growing income stream.

Some people build entire micro-niche websites around one category—like kitchen gadgets or home office gear. Others make curated "Best Of" lists—Best Budget Cameras, Best Planner Tools, etc. These assets work for you 24/7, and once indexed by Google or Pinterest, they generate ongoing traffic without ongoing effort.

Affiliate marketing, when treated seriously, is not just a hustle. It can become a business. One that earns money while you're on vacation, sleeping, or working on your next project.

4.

Creating & Flipping Simple Websites or Domains

There's a quiet thrill in building something small that turns into something valuable. Unlike traditional businesses, which often take months or years to become profitable, website and domain flipping gives you a chance to build quick digital assets and cash in faster than most people realize. If you've ever wanted to make money from thin air—without holding products, dealing with customers, or even being a web expert—this hustle is a hidden gem. At its core, website and domain flipping is about creating or acquiring something undervalued, improving it just enough to make it more attractive, and then reselling it for a profit. It's the real estate of the digital world—but you don't need to be rich to get started. You just need to be clever, observant, and willing to learn.

Flipping websites or domains is often misunderstood as something only tech-savvy entrepreneurs or coders can do. But in reality, anyone who understands what people are searching for and what businesses need to grow can thrive in this space. The entry cost can be under $20, and the upside? Limitless. There are people making thousands of dollars flipping simple one-page websites, and others who've turned domain purchases into five-figure exits. And the best part? You can start tonight—with nothing but a browser, a few hours of effort, and some strategic thinking.

Domain Flipping: The Simpler Gateway

Let's start with the lighter lift: domain flipping. This hustle is almost poetic in its simplicity. You buy a domain name (a .com, .net, or .co, etc.) that you think might be valuable to someone else—either now or in the future—and then you sell it at a higher price. Think of it like buying land in a part of town that's not developed yet. You get it cheap because no one else sees the value—yet.

The key here is to anticipate demand. What kind of businesses might pop up next year? What trends are taking off? Are there new buzzwords, slang, or brands that could become popular? Timing and intuition are everything. For instance, imagine buying "AIContentTools.com" just before the artificial intelligence boom, or "VeganMealKits.com" just before a plant-based trend hit mainstream. These kinds of names can sell for hundreds or even thousands of dollars later.

You can register a domain using platforms like:

- Namecheap
- GoDaddy
- Google Domains
- Dynadot

After securing the domain, you can either list it for sale immediately (on sites like Sedo, Flippa, or Afternic), or hold onto it while its potential value grows. It's digital land speculation—but far more accessible. You don't need permits, lawyers, or inspections. You just need the vision.

The emotional rush of getting your first domain sale is like magic. One day you bought something for $10. A week, month, or year later, someone pays you $200 or more because they need it for their new business. You realize: you just created value out of an idea.

Website Flipping: Digital Homes with a Purpose

If domain flipping is buying land, website flipping is developing the house. It's the next level up—not much more complicated, but with greater rewards. You start with either a brand-new site or an underperforming existing one, improve it, and sell it to someone who wants a shortcut into the online business world. Most people think building websites is reserved for programmers or designers, but with today's tools like WordPress, Carrd, Wix, Webflow, and Shopify, that simply isn't true.

One of the smartest overnight hustles is building a simple one-page niche website with content, a lead magnet, or an affiliate link, and then selling it to a business or entrepreneur who wants a ready-to-go web presence. These "starter sites" often sell for anywhere between $200 and $2,000, depending on their quality, design, and niche. Even a basic "plumber in Dallas" landing page or "dog walker booking site" with placeholder text can attract small business owners who don't have time to build from scratch.

There's a massive emotional satisfaction in knowing that you've built something functional, even if it's small. You get to play both creator and entrepreneur. And when someone buys it from you, they're often thanking you for saving them time, money, and stress.

Subtopic: What Kind of Websites Can You Flip?

This is where things get exciting, because the possibilities are endless. You can flip:

- Local Business Templates – Generic sites for dentists, landscapers, cleaners, etc.
- Affiliate Niche Sites – Focused on one product type (like ergonomic chairs or hiking backpacks).
- Newsletter or Blog Sites – Built with a content plan and a few sample posts.
- Service Booking Sites – Set up for people offering one service (photography, tutoring, dog walking).
- Dropshipping Stores – Shopify or WooCommerce stores preloaded with products and branding.

You don't have to fill them with much—just enough to show the idea. A homepage, an about page, a contact form, maybe a blog post or two. Think of it like staging a house. The point is to help someone see the vision.

Where to Sell Your Websites or Domains

Once you've created your website or secured a few domain names, the next step is finding buyers. Here's where to list your digital real estate:

- Flippa.com – The biggest marketplace for buying and selling websites, domains, and online businesses.
- EmpireFlippers.com – Higher quality listings, but they vet websites more strictly.
- Sedo.com – Great for domain flipping specifically.
- Facebook groups & Subreddits – Look for communities like "Website Flipping" or "Buy & Sell Online Businesses."
- Private Outreach – Find small business owners in need of a website, and pitch your ready-to-go site directly.

You'd be amazed at how many small business owners are too busy or overwhelmed to build their own site. If you can offer them something semi-customized, clean, and functional, they'll gladly pay for the convenience.

How to Build a Website in One Night

If you're reading this book, chances are you want to start tonight. So here's how to build a flip-worthy site in just a few hours:

1. Choose a niche or purpose. Keep it simple: a tutoring service, a photography portfolio, or a niche blog.
2. Pick a platform. For beginners, Carrd.co or Wix.com are perfect. WordPress is great too, especially with free themes.
3. Buy a domain. Connect it to your site or use a subdomain for now.

4. Add content. Use AI or write 2–3 pages of basic copy: Home, About, Services, Contact. Make it feel real, even if fictional.

5. Include visuals. Use free stock images from sites like Pexels or Unsplash.

6. Publish it. That's it. You now have a digital asset ready for flipping.

You don't need to overthink it. The goal is to show possibility. And once you do this once, you'll realize how repeatable it is.

The Emotional Journey: From Clicks to Cash

There's something deeply satisfying about watching a $9 domain flip for $300, or seeing a simple website you made in your bedroom go on to become someone's full-fledged business site. This hustle is part creativity, part timing, and part guts. You're not just selling pixels—you're selling potential. You're giving people a shortcut to their dreams, and getting paid for it.

Many people go their whole lives without realizing how easy it is to create value digitally. They think you have to invent an app or code a platform. But flipping websites proves that you can be a digital craftsman without needing a tech degree. All it takes is effort, resourcefulness, and belief in your ideas.

Scaling This Hustle

Once you've done your first flip—whether it's a domain or a website—it's time to go bigger. You can:

- Build bundles of niche sites and sell them as a package

- Team up with content writers or designers to create premium sites
- Start a small agency offering "starter websites" to entrepreneurs
- Combine affiliate marketing with your flipped sites for passive income

Some flippers build 5–10 simple websites a month, list them all, and sell 2–3 steadily. Over time, this can grow into a six-figure business, all from home.

5.

Online Tutoring or Language Lessons

There's something powerful about sharing what you know. Knowledge, after all, is one of the few things that increases the more you give it away. And in a world where millions of people are hungry to learn—from school subjects to new languages to life skills—offering online tutoring or lessons can become not just a hustle, but a mission. What's more, it's a hustle you can launch tonight, even with nothing but a smartphone, a Zoom account, and confidence in what you know. Whether you're tutoring algebra, teaching Spanish, or showing someone how to write a better resume, this hustle offers immediate demand, emotional connection, and strong earning potential.

Why Online Tutoring Works So Well Right Now

The post-pandemic world has redefined how people learn. Online education is no longer a niche—it's a norm. Parents want extra help for their kids. Adults want to upgrade their skills. Immigrants want to learn local languages. Professionals want to get certified. In all of these areas, you can position yourself as a bridge between frustration and confidence. And the best part? You don't need to be a licensed teacher to get started.

If you've ever gotten good grades in school, helped a friend study, or explained something clearly, you're already halfway qualified. The rest is just packaging what you know into a valuable service. Platforms like Wyzant, Preply, Cambly, Superprof, or even Craigslist and Facebook groups can help you find clients quickly. Or, if you're feeling bold, you can launch your own independent tutoring business using Zoom, Calendly, and PayPal.

What Can You Teach Tonight?

This is where the doors swing wide open. You don't need to teach calculus or advanced physics (unless you want to). People are searching for help in a wide range of subjects:

- Academic tutoring: Math, science, English, writing, history
- Test prep: SAT, ACT, GRE, GMAT, IELTS, TOEFL
- Languages: English, Spanish, French, Mandarin, etc.
- Business skills: Public speaking, writing, using Excel or PowerPoint
- Creative skills: Music, drawing, photography, editing
- Life and career coaching:. Resume writing, college essays, job interviews

You don't need to know everything. You just need to know more than the person you're helping—and be willing to listen, encourage, and adapt. That human touch goes further than you think.

How to Get Your First Client Tonight

Here's a simple formula:

1. Pick your subject. Choose what you're most confident in. Start narrow. For example, "high school algebra homework help."
2. Create a profile or listing. Go on a site like Preply, Wyzant, or even Fiverr and describe your service.
3. Reach out directly. Post in Facebook groups, parent forums, or language exchange boards. Be honest, friendly, and offer a free 15-minute trial.
4. Use what you have. A basic webcam and a quiet room are enough to start. Use Zoom or Google Meet. No fancy tools required.
5. Set a low price to start. Something like \$10–\$15/hour helps you build reviews fast. Then raise your rate as demand grows.

The emotional reward of helping someone finally understand a topic they've struggled with is priceless. You're not just making money—you're making someone's life easier.

Building Trust Through Teaching

One of the most underrated skills in the hustle world is empathy. When you tutor someone, you're not just sharing knowledge—you're building trust. That moment when a student says, "Oh! I get it now!" is like a dopamine rush. It reminds you why this hustle matters. You're giving someone confidence. You're helping them pass a test, speak to their in-laws, or get a new job. You become a guide—not just a gig worker.

This trust turns into repeat business, referrals, and better pay. Many tutors start at $15/hour but eventually charge $40, $60, or even $100/hour for specialized services. Parents especially are willing to invest when they know their child is improving. Adults are loyal to tutors who make them feel smart, not stupid.

Going Beyond One-on-One

Once you've got a few clients, you can scale this hustle in creative ways:

- Group sessions: Teach 3–5 people at once and earn more per hour.
- Recorded lessons: Turn your most popular sessions into YouTube videos or paid courses on Udemy.
- Workbooks or PDFs: Sell your own study guides or cheat sheets.
- Language clubs or study groups: Create communities that meet weekly for a fee.
- Suddenly, you're not just a tutor—you're an educator with a brand. That's powerful.

Real Life, Real Emotions

I once knew a college student who tutored kids in math to help pay for his rent. He started on Craigslist, charging $10 an hour. Within six months, he had ten clients, a waiting list, and was charging $40/hour. But more than that, he had parents texting him grateful messages, kids who looked up to him, and a newfound sense of purpose. What started as a hustle turned into a calling.

That can be your story, too. You don't need credentials to begin. You need heart, patience, and the guts to put yourself out there. If you've ever helped a friend understand something better, you've already taken the first step. Now it's time to turn that into a hustle that not only pays—but lifts others as it lifts you.

6.

Publishing

Of all the hustles in this book, this one is my personal favorite. Publishing has changed my life. It has taken me from staring at a blank screen, wondering how to survive the next month, to waking up with gratitude and $10,000 in my account from one month's royalties. And I did it without a fancy publisher, a degree in literature, or even much startup money. Just grit, a laptop, and the willingness to learn how to turn my words into a product. If you're looking for a hustle that rewards creativity, builds passive income, and lets you reach people all over the world from the comfort of your home, publishing might just be your calling too.

Why Publishing Is More Than a Hustle

Most people think writing a book is for authors with agents, contracts, and years of experience. But today, anyone can write, publish, and profit from their own books. Platforms like Amazon Kindle Direct Publishing (KDP), IngramSpark, Kobo, Barnes & Noble Press, and Draft2Digital (D2D) have torn down the gates and handed you the keys. These platforms give you the tools to reach readers across the globe without ever needing a warehouse or a publishing deal. All you need is a manuscript, a book cover, and a willingness to hit "publish."

And here's the thing: the barrier to entry is low, but the rewards can be massive. Publishing a book isn't just a one-time gig—it's a product that can earn for years. You can sell eBooks, paperbacks, audiobooks, and even hardcovers. You can go wide across multiple platforms or stay exclusive to Amazon and benefit from their massive traffic and promotional tools. It's a business. It's a hustle. And for me, it became a calling.

The Platforms That Make It Happen

Let's break down the platforms that helped me earn—and how they can do the same for you.

1. Amazon KDP (Kindle Direct Publishing)

This is the giant. Amazon owns over 70% of the eBook market. Publishing on KDP is free. You upload your manuscript, choose your price, and Amazon takes care of the rest. Your book goes live worldwide in 72 hours or less.

How they pay:

- Royalties range from 35% to 70% depending on the pricing and region.
- Payments are monthly, typically 60 days after the sale month.

Pros:

- Huge traffic and customer base
- No upfront cost
- Print-on-demand paperbacks
- Amazon Ads and Kindle Unlimited bonuses

Cons:

- You're competing with millions of books
- Amazon can be strict with rules (e.g., duplicate content)
- Some niches are saturated

But if you do it right—and I'll help you do it right—you can build a strong, consistent income stream here. This book you're reading? You probably found it through Amazon.

2. IngramSpark

IngramSpark is ideal if you want wide distribution. They get your book into libraries, indie bookstores, and international markets.

How they pay:

- Royalties vary, usually 45% or more, minus printing costs
- Payments are monthly with a delay similar to Amazon

Pros:

- Global reach in libraries and stores
- Hardcover options
- Professional-looking distribution

Cons:

- Has setup fees (waived during promos or with codes)
- Can be a bit technical to use

It's not a beginner's platform—but once you get the hang of Amazon, moving into IngramSpark is a natural step if you want legitimacy and long-term scaling.

3. Kobo Writing Life

Kobo is a solid platform especially in Canada, Europe, and Asia. Great for reaching readers who don't use Amazon.

How they pay:

- 70% royalties for books priced $2.99 and up
- Monthly payouts

Pros:

- Clean interface
- Friendly to authors
- Wide international audience

Cons:

- Smaller market than Amazon
- Requires marketing effort to drive sales

4. Barnes & Noble Press

If you've ever dreamed of seeing your book in an actual bookstore, this is a way in. B&N Press is easy to use and directly connects you with their online and brick-and-mortar stores.

How they pay:

- 55% royalties for print books, 65% for eBooks
- Monthly payments

Pros:

- Trusted brand
- High-quality print options
- No exclusivity required

Cons:

- Less traffic than Amazon
- Print books need strong formatting

5. Draft2Digital (D2D)

D2D is the ultimate time-saver. It distributes your book to Apple Books, Kobo, Barnes & Noble, and more—all from one dashboard.

How they pay:

- Takes about 10% commission on royalties
- Monthly payments

Pros:

- Wide distribution
- Converts your manuscript into professional formats
- User-friendly

Cons:

- Not ideal for Amazon (you should upload there separately)
- Limited print distribution compared to IngramSpark

Why This Hustle is My Favorite

I'll be real with you. This hustle gave me hope when I had none. I've made over $10,000 in a single month from books—books I wrote, formatted, designed covers for, and uploaded myself. No team. No big investment. Just passion and persistence.

It started slow. My first book barely made $50. But I kept learning. I found niches. I tested titles, covers, and keywords. I studied what readers wanted. I reinvested every dollar into better designs and more research. And now, I wake up to passive income every day.

I believe in this hustle so much that if you need help—any help—I want you to contact me directly. Whether it's your manuscript, your book cover, your formatting, or just figuring out what to write about, I will personally support you. Reach out to me at:

princephoenix959@gmail.com
danieldavidphoenix@gmail.com

You're not in this alone. This isn't just a chapter. This is an open door.

How to Get Started Tonight

Here's a simple roadmap:

1. Choose a niche. Think about what you know or what people want to learn. Need help picking? Email me—I'll help you find it.

2. Write your manuscript. It doesn't have to be perfect. It just has to be helpful or entertaining.

3. Design a cover. Use Canva or hire someone cheap on Fiverr—or ask me.

4. Format it. Use tools like Reedsy or D2D's free formatter.

5. Upload it. Start with Amazon KDP, then expand to others.

6. Promote it. Use Facebook groups, TikTok, blogs, or even Amazon ads.

And just like that, you're a published author. You've got a product that can pay you for years.

Subtopic: Evergreen vs. Trendy Books

If you want longevity, aim for "evergreen" topics—books people will need forever: how-tos, self-help, motivation, skills, cooking, parenting. But don't ignore trends either. I've made great money from timely books about AI tools, crypto, and new apps. Mix both to keep cash flowing.

The Emotional High of Impact

There's nothing like the message from a stranger saying, "Your book changed me." That's the kind of impact no job title can buy. Your story, your lessons, your creativity—it matters. When you hit publish, you give the world a piece of yourself. And when someone chooses your book from millions, that's a feeling of validation and joy like no other.

Final Word

This chapter is more than a hustle guide. It's a testimony. Publishing has been my ladder out of financial struggle, self-doubt, and fear. It's not just about making money—it's about building something real. Something you can point to. Something that lasts.

You can do this. And if you need help, I'm here. Let me be the person I wish I had when I started. Let's publish your first book. Let's make this hustle work for you.

Part II: Physical Hustles That Pay Quickly

7.

Flipping Items from Home or Thrift Stores

There's something magical about turning clutter into cash. About digging through a dusty shelf, finding something that looks like junk to the average eye, and recognizing it for what it truly is: a treasure. This hustle—flipping items from your home or thrift stores—isn't just about making quick money. It's about seeing hidden value, about sharpening your instincts, and learning how to turn knowledge into profit. It's the art of resale, and it's one of the fastest ways to go from zero to income by tomorrow.

Let's face it, most of us have way more stuff than we need. Tucked away in closets, storage bins, garages, or attics are items we once loved, used, or just bought on impulse. Things we've forgotten, or things we always meant to sell "someday." That someday is now. Because every unused item in your home is untapped potential. It's money sitting on a shelf. The same goes for thrift stores. Most people walk right past value because they don't know what to look for—but once you train your eye, a $2 item can become $30 in your pocket. And when you multiply that, flipping can turn into a serious income stream.

Why Flipping Works Overnight

The beauty of flipping is its immediacy. You don't need a website, a business license, or a large following to get started. All you need is an internet connection, a place to list your item (like Facebook Marketplace, eBay, OfferUp, Craigslist, or Mercari), and something to sell. And chances are, you already have something in your home that someone else would pay good money for.

Flipping isn't just a hustle; it's a mindset. It's about shifting the way you look at your belongings, and the world around you. It's realizing that people will pay for things you no longer need: the old iPhone box in your drawer, the shoes you wore once, the record player that's gathering dust, or the vintage backpack you found for $5 at Goodwill. Once you start seeing with those eyes, you won't be able to stop.

Start at Home: The No-Cost Inventory

The first place to start is right where you are. You don't need to spend a dollar to get started. Walk through your house as if you were a buyer, not an owner. Open every drawer. Look at your shelves, closets, garage, kitchen cabinets. What haven't you touched in six months? What could be valuable to someone else?

Look for electronics, books, brand-name clothes, shoes, collectibles, small kitchen appliances, gaming accessories, or anything new in the box. Items with original packaging or instruction manuals often sell faster and for higher prices. Even random stuff like remote controls, empty Apple boxes, or discontinued cosmetics have markets you wouldn't believe. The trick is to not judge the item by whether you'd buy it—but whether someone else might want it.

Once you've gathered a few items, research their value. Use eBay's "sold listings" feature to see what similar items have recently sold for. This helps you price competitively. From there, take clear, well-lit photos of your item from different angles. Write an honest but appealing description. Post it to multiple platforms. And wait—though not usually for long.

The Power of Thrift Stores

When you've flipped through your own inventory and want more, thrift stores become your treasure maps. Thrift shops, garage sales, flea markets, and clearance racks are gold mines when you know what to look for. Go in with a budget—$20 is enough to start—and an open mind. Look for recognizable brands, vintage items, or anything quirky and rare.

At first, it can be overwhelming. You might not know what has value. That's okay. Take your phone with you and Google items in the store. Use barcode scanner apps or search eBay to compare. Over time, you'll get a feel for what sells quickly. Some of the best flips are unexpected: vintage Pyrex bowls, old cameras, branded sneakers, first-edition books, designer bags, retro electronics, or even high-end board games.

The best part? Thrift store flipping often comes with huge margins. A $4 hoodie can sell for $35. A $1 VHS tape can fetch $20. A $3 coffee maker might go for $40. These are real numbers, and I've seen them again and again.

Platforms to Sell On

- Not all platforms are created equal, and knowing where to list can make a big difference.
- Facebook Marketplace: Great for local pickups. No shipping required. Fast cash. Best for furniture, tools, home goods, and bulky items.
- eBay: Ideal for collectibles, electronics, vintage items, and brand-name goods. Offers global reach.
- Mercari: Simple to use. Better for fashion, beauty, and general home items.
- Poshmark: Best for clothes, shoes, and accessories.
- OfferUp: Good for local deals, similar to Facebook Marketplace.

Use cross-listing tools like List Perfectly or Vendoo if you want to save time by posting the same item to multiple platforms.

Pricing with Purpose

Pricing is both an art and a science. You want to be competitive, but you also want to make a profit. Start by looking at the "sold" price of similar items. Consider shipping and platform fees (eBay takes around 13%, Mercari around 10%). Then ask: how quickly do you want to sell?

If you're looking for fast flips, price on the lower end of the market range. If you're patient and believe the item is rare or valuable, price it higher and wait. You can always drop the price later. Also, don't forget the power of negotiation. On local platforms, always price a little higher than your lowest acceptable price. People love to haggle.

Subtopic: Mistakes to Avoid

Let me save you from some hard lessons I learned early on. Don't skip on research. Don't assume something has value—check the sold listings. Don't post blurry, dark photos or vague descriptions. Don't ignore shipping costs. And never misrepresent an item. If there's damage, say so. Honesty builds trust and repeat buyers.

Also, don't hoard inventory. It's easy to buy more than you sell. Keep your space manageable and stay focused on moving what you have before stocking up too heavily.

The Emotional Side of the Flip

There's a thrill in flipping. Every sale is a little victory. A reminder that you created value out of something someone else overlooked. You start to feel empowered. You realize you don't need a 9-to-5 to earn. You just need creativity, effort, and the willingness to try.

It also teaches you to see the world differently. That clutter is cash. That people want things you take for granted. That every trip to a thrift store or a yard sale is a treasure hunt. It's not just about the money—it's about learning to see possibilities in unexpected places.

And let's be honest, there's something deeply satisfying about turning a $3 investment into $30. Or about seeing a product you found in a dusty bin now proudly displayed in someone's home. You're not just selling stuff. You're matching stories with new owners.

Turning Flipping Into a Business

Once you've gotten a taste of success, you might want to scale. That's where things get fun. Create a simple system to track your profits. Consider reinvesting your profits into better gear—like a ring light for better photos, or a thermal label printer for faster shipping. Some flippers even create niche stores: vintage books, branded sneakers, retro toys. Specializing helps you become an expert, and customers will start to seek you out.

You can also go beyond flipping physical items. Source liquidation pallets. Partner with thrift shops. Resell clearance items from retail stores. Use cashback and rewards apps to boost margins. There are entire communities online dedicated to reselling. Join them. Learn. Grow.

Final Words: From Hustle to Habit

I've met people who paid off debt with flipping. I've met single parents who used this hustle to put food on the table. I've met teens who turned flipping sneakers into six-figure incomes. And I've done it myself when I needed quick money without any gatekeepers.

Flipping works. It's fast. It's tangible. And it can become more than just a hustle. It can be a skill you carry for life—a way of seeing value where others don't. So tonight, don't just scroll on your phone. Open that closet. Visit that thrift store. Pick something, price it, post it, and see what happens.

Because your next $100 might already be sitting right in front of you.

8.

Same-Day Delivery and Gig Apps (DoorDash, Uber Eats, etc.)

There's something deeply motivating about knowing you can make money today—not next week, not after some long application process, but within hours. That's the power of the gig economy. In a world that's more connected and fast-paced than ever, people are ordering food, groceries, packages, and convenience at an all-time high. And behind that demand are hustlers—people like you—who are seizing the opportunity to turn their time, vehicles, and energy into fast, reliable cash. Whether it's DoorDash, Uber Eats, Instacart, Amazon Flex, or other on-demand apps, the same-day delivery hustle is one of the most accessible ways to start making real money tonight.

The Power of Signing Up and Showing Up

One of the most beautiful aspects of the delivery gig world is how quickly you can jump in. Most apps require just a few things: a background check, a valid driver's license, a decent vehicle (sometimes even a bike or scooter works), and a smartphone. In many cities, you can sign up in the morning, get approved by the afternoon, and be on the road that evening delivering tacos, groceries, or packages. There's no interview, no resume, no waiting for someone to decide you're worth hiring. You decide. You show up. And you get paid.

For anyone who's ever felt shut out of opportunity, that's incredibly empowering. Maybe you've been laid off. Maybe your resume's outdated. Maybe you're in between jobs or just need to boost your income quickly. Gig apps don't ask about your past—they only care if you can get the job done today. That's what makes them such powerful tools for those of us ready to hustle.

Choosing the Right App for You

Each delivery platform has its quirks, pros, and downsides. Let's break down the main ones so you can decide where to start based on what works best for your area, schedule, and goals.

DoorDash: One of the most popular food delivery platforms, available in most cities and suburbs. Easy to sign up. Offers incentives like Peak Pay during busy hours. Allows for flexible scheduling or immediate dashing.

Uber Eats: Great if you're already driving for Uber, or if you want to deliver both food and passengers. In some areas, you can do both from the same app. Tips can be generous.

Instacart: Focused on grocery delivery. You'll be shopping and delivering, so it takes longer than simple food drop-offs, but often pays more per batch. Excellent in suburban areas with large grocery stores.

Amazon Flex: Ideal if you want structure. You claim delivery blocks and deliver Amazon packages from local warehouses. Requires more commitment and scheduling, but offers predictable payouts.

Grubhub and Postmates: Still active in many areas. Worth signing up if they're big in your city.

If you're in a dense urban area, you might even consider doing deliveries on a bike or scooter. Apps like Uber Eats and DoorDash offer this option and it can save you money on gas while getting some exercise too.

Getting Set Up to Deliver Fast

Before you hit the road, make sure you're set up for success. Start by creating a delivery "go bag." This should include:

- A phone charger and power bank (your battery will drain quickly)
- Insulated delivery bags for hot/cold items
- A dash mount for your phone
- Hand sanitizer and napkins
- Water and snacks for yourself

Download all the necessary apps, turn on notifications, and familiarize yourself with the layout. Most apps will walk you through tutorials, but it helps to watch a few YouTube videos for real-world tips. Join local Facebook groups or Reddit threads for your area's drivers—these communities are gold for understanding hotspots, safety tips, and how to maximize bonuses.

The First Day on the Job

The first delivery is a rush. You feel like a secret agent with a mission: pick up the goods, deliver to the right address, and get a tip. It's thrilling and surprisingly satisfying. But it can also be awkward—parking can be tricky, instructions unclear, or restaurants backed up.

Stay patient. Stay calm. Each order is a learning experience. Communicate clearly through the app if you're delayed. Take photos as proof of delivery when required. Always double-check the order. And don't let a bad experience throw you off. The learning curve is short, and confidence builds quickly.

By the end of your first few hours, you'll have a rhythm. You'll start recognizing which restaurants are fast, which neighborhoods tip better, and which times of day are busiest. That knowledge is power—and it will help you start optimizing quickly.

How Much Can You Make?

Let's talk numbers. On average, drivers report making anywhere from $15–$25 per hour with gig delivery, depending on tips, location, and timing. If you stack bonuses, Peak Pay, and batch deliveries (like Instacart or Amazon Flex), you can boost that number.

Your income depends on:

- When you drive (lunch/dinner rush pays more)
- Where you drive (urban areas usually have higher volume)
- How efficiently you deliver (avoid long wait times or low-paying orders)
- Tips (some customers tip generously, some don't tip at all)

Some drivers hustle hard during weekends or big events (like Super Bowl Sunday or New Year's Eve) and pull in $200–$400 in a day. Others treat it like a part-time side hustle to make $50–$100 in a few hours after work. You choose your grind.

The Emotional Journey of Delivery Work

At first glance, delivery might seem like a simple trade: time for money. But when you get out there and start doing it, something else happens. You meet people. You see neighborhoods you've never explored. You get to witness small moments—like a kid's face lighting up at a pizza delivery or a tired mom thanking you for bringing her groceries. You become a part of the everyday rhythm of people's lives.

And you start to feel something more profound: independence. Pride. You're not waiting for someone to give you a break. You're taking one. You're out there in the real world, exchanging value for money, on your terms. You control your hours. You decide how hard you work. There's a freedom in that that's hard to describe until you've lived it.

And when the money starts stacking up, when you realize you've paid for gas, groceries, or rent from your hustle—that's when it hits. You did this. You didn't just sit around hoping. You moved.

Strategies to Maximize Earnings

If you want to move beyond just earning pocket change and turn this into a serious income, you need strategy.

Multi-App: Use more than one app at once. If DoorDash is slow, Uber Eats might be hot. Stack them.

Know Your Zones: Learn where the demand is strongest. Park near clusters of restaurants, college campuses, or office parks.

Optimize Timing: Lunch (11 AM–2 PM) and dinner (5 PM–9 PM) are peak times. Weekend evenings are gold.

Track Your Miles: Use an app like Stride or Hurdlr to log your expenses and mileage for tax write-offs.

Decline Low Offers: Don't accept every order. $3 to drive 6 miles? Decline. Time is money.

Batch Orders: Some apps let you deliver multiple orders in one trip—maximize that.

Burnout is Real—Protect Your Sanity

Like any hustle, the risk of burnout is real. Long hours on the road, dealing with traffic, rude customers, or unresponsive support can wear you down. That's why balance is key.

Take breaks. Listen to music or audiobooks while driving. Set daily income goals and stop once you hit them. Celebrate small wins. And remember your "why"—whether it's paying off debt, buying a gift for your kid, or building freedom.

You're not just delivering food. You're delivering for yourself. Keep that in your heart.

Final Words: From First Tip to Financial Transformation

There's something beautiful about the first time you get a tip notification. A stranger just gave you money because you showed up. That feeling—that validation—is electric. And it doesn't fade. Whether you're doing it for a night or making a full-time income, this hustle puts the power back in your hands.

So sign up. Show up. Turn the key in your ignition, and go chase that bag. Because out there, someone's hungry, someone's busy, someone's grateful—and they're willing to pay. And here you are, ready to answer the call.

You don't need permission. You don't need perfection. You just need drive—literally and figuratively. And tonight, that drive can take you farther than you think.

9.

Renting Out What You Own (Car, Room, Equipment)

Have you ever looked around your home and wondered how much untapped money might be sitting in plain sight? That old bicycle leaning against the garage wall. The guest room that hasn't seen a visitor in months. The leaf blower collecting dust. The car that's paid off and parked more often than not. In today's economy—where quick cash can mean the difference between peace of mind and sleepless nights—learning how to rent out what you already own might just be one of the most powerful, overlooked hustles out there. It's not about starting something new from scratch. It's about unlocking income from the things you already have. And believe me when I say, there's power in that. Deep, transformative power.

Let's start with one of the biggest money-makers: your car. You may think your car is just a way to get from Point A to Point B, but in the right context, it's an asset that could earn you hundreds—sometimes even thousands—each month. Platforms like Turo, Getaround, and HyreCar allow you to rent out your vehicle on your terms. Whether it's for a day, a weekend, or longer, people are constantly searching for flexible, affordable transportation options, and your car could be the perfect solution. With Turo, for instance, you list your vehicle, select availability, approve guests (if desired), and earn money every time it's rented. The best part? Turo offers liability coverage and customer support, so you're not left hanging if something goes wrong. It's passive income with protection—a combination that's hard to beat.

But what if you're worried about your car getting damaged? That's valid. Turo provides up to $750,000 in liability insurance, and they offer a range of protection plans to choose from. You can also set parameters around mileage and rental conditions. And the truth is, many car owners who feared the worst quickly found that the risk is minimal and the reward is worth it. One single weekend rental could bring in what you'd earn working several part-time shifts. That's time you get back for yourself or for your family. That's stress lifted off your shoulders. That's the beginning of financial breathing room.

If you live in an urban area or near a tourist spot, the demand for rentals is even higher. And don't forget about Getaround, which automates bookings with keyless car access. That means you don't even have to meet renters in person. Once it's set up, it runs almost entirely on autopilot. This is especially powerful if you have a second vehicle or if you're working from home and not using your car daily. Instead of watching it depreciate, you're watching it earn.

Now, let's shift gears and talk about something even more accessible: your living space. Airbnb, Vrbo, and similar platforms have completely changed the way people travel. You no longer need to own an entire property to make money in real estate. That spare room? That finished basement? Even a well-furnished living room with a pull-out couch can become a money-maker overnight. With Airbnb, you create a listing, upload some clear photos, write a welcoming description, and set your availability. It's that simple. And in many cities, guests are willing to pay top dollar for a cozy, affordable alternative to hotels.

What's beautiful about this hustle is how flexible it is. You decide when your space is available. Maybe it's only on weekends when you visit family. Maybe it's during peak holidays when demand spikes. Maybe it's while you're on vacation, turning your empty house into a cash machine. And you control the rules. Want a two-night minimum? Set it. No pets allowed? Specify it. Airbnb's platform is built to support hosts with pricing tools, guest reviews, and up to $1 million in damage protection. You're not going at it alone.

And for those who feel uneasy about hosting strangers, that's completely understandable. But there are ways to ease into it. Start by renting to guests with strong reviews. Use lockboxes or smart locks to minimize face-to-face interaction. Or, if the idea still doesn't sit right, consider platforms like Neighbor.com. This site allows you to rent out storage space in your home—your attic, your garage, even an empty closet—to people who need it. No guests, no cleaning, no awkward check-ins. Just passive income from unused square footage. You'd be surprised how many people are looking for affordable storage solutions, especially in crowded cities.

Now, let's dive into a lesser-known but incredibly profitable avenue: renting out your equipment. Maybe you've got a DSLR camera from your photography phase, or a power drill from that one time you tried building a deck. These items are valuable—not just to you, but to people who need them temporarily. Platforms like Fat Llama, Loanables, and ShareGrid connect you with renters in your area looking for tools, tech, and gear. Think about that: your equipment earning money while you do nothing. You don't have to sell it. You don't have to work it. You just make it available.

The range of rentable items is staggering. Ladders, pressure washers, projectors, musical instruments, event chairs, lighting kits—you name it. Every item sitting idle is a missed opportunity. Even gaming consoles and camping gear can bring in consistent income. You'll be amazed how much people will pay to borrow instead of buy. And with built-in insurance options, you're covered if something goes wrong.

This model of hustling—renting instead of selling—has another incredible benefit: sustainability. You're helping reduce waste and encouraging shared resources. That's not just good for your wallet—it's good for your conscience. You're part of a movement that values smart use over needless consumption. And let's face it, that feels good.

But let's talk real numbers. You don't need dozens of items to make this work. Let's say you list your second car on Turo and it rents just six days a month at $50 per day. That's $300. Now add your guest room on Airbnb for weekends only—maybe two nights a week at $80 per night. That's $640.

Now throw in a couple of tools or a camera rented a few times a month for $30 each. That's another $90. Altogether, you're looking at over $1,000 a month. That's rent money. That's bill money. That's breathing room.

And for those who say, "But I don't have anything people would want to rent," I challenge you: make a list. Walk around your home. Look in closets, garages, and drawers. You'll be surprised. That spare monitor? Someone needs it. That ladder? It's gold for weekend warriors. That old tent? Perfect for a family going camping once. You don't have to have everything—you just need to offer something.

This hustle is close to my heart. I've seen people change their entire financial picture by renting out what they already own. I've helped others list their first item, and I've seen the smile when their first payment came in. This very book you're reading was funded—at least in part—by income generated from this exact hustle. That's how real this is. And if you ever need help getting started, from creating listings to setting pricing, from writing descriptions to choosing the right platforms, reach out to me.
I've helped people with book covers, manuscripts, coaching, and getting started with side income, and I'd be honored to help you too. If you're stuck, if you need niches, if you want someone to take a look at your setup—I'm here.

Remember, this is about taking control. It's about no longer waiting for someone else to give you permission to earn. It's about realizing that what you have is enough to begin. Not tomorrow. Not next month. Now. The gig economy isn't just for drivers or coders—it's for anyone who's willing to look around and say, "What can I offer today?"

So get started. Take photos. Write a listing. Press publish. And let your stuff start working for you.

10.

Local Odd Jobs: Handywork, Yard Work, or Cleaning

Sometimes the best money is made with your two hands and a little sweat. In a world buzzing with digital opportunities, we often overlook the old-school, tried-and-true way of earning: helping our neighbors, one job at a time. Whether it's mowing a lawn, fixing a leaky faucet, hauling junk, or deep cleaning a garage, local odd jobs are a goldmine hiding in plain sight. It's humble work, but it's honest—and often, it pays immediately.

What makes this hustle beautiful is its accessibility. You don't need a website, you don't need a degree, and you don't need a thousand followers. You just need the willingness to serve. In fact, if you've ever helped someone move, cleaned your own apartment, or done a bit of home maintenance, you're already qualified.

Why Local Odd Jobs Work So Well

Let's start with the obvious: people are busy. They're overwhelmed. They're tired. They'd rather pay someone to mow the lawn, clean out the gutters, or assemble furniture than do it themselves. That's where you come in. These are jobs that fall through the cracks of busy modern life, and they often pay better than expected—especially when the alternative for your customer is hiring a pricey contractor or service.

There's a personal element to this hustle that other jobs lack. When you work locally, you're not just a username or a gig ID. You're a real person showing up on someone's doorstep. You build trust quickly. Word spreads. You might start by cleaning one house, but next week, it's their sister, their coworker, their neighbor. One job turns into a network.

Where to Find Jobs Fast

Start close to home. Ask family, friends, and neighbors if they need anything done. Tell them you're available for odd jobs—yard work, repairs, deep cleaning, organizing, pet cleanup, you name it. Most people have a chore they've been putting off. You just became their solution.

From there, branch out. Post in local Facebook groups, community apps like Nextdoor, and on Craigslist under the "services" section. Use language like:

"Reliable and affordable help with yard work, moving, junk removal, and more! Available this weekend. Message me for details!"

Use photos if possible—before-and-after shots of work you've done, even in your own home. Visual proof builds credibility. Offer a first-time discount to get your foot in the door.

Another powerful move: visit local businesses or homes and drop off a flyer or card. Especially in older neighborhoods, where people may not be as tech-savvy, a simple knock on the door or a friendly smile goes a long way. Make sure your contact info is clear and your message simple.

Pricing Your Work

This part can be tricky at first. You want to be fair to yourself, but you don't want to scare people off. A good starting point for general labor is $20–$30 an hour, more if the job is dirty or requires tools. For flat-rate work, like cleaning a garage, hauling trash, or doing yard work, estimate how long it will take and what effort is involved.

Here's a tip: under-promise, over-deliver. Say the job will take three hours, then finish in two and a half. Price yourself in the middle of the market, but deliver top-tier service. People remember that. It's what turns one-time work into steady income.

If someone tries to lowball you, be respectful but firm. You're not just charging for time—you're charging for reliability, skill, and effort. And if you don't value your time, no one else will either.

Tools of the Trade

You don't need a truckload of equipment, but a few basic tools go a long way: a sturdy rake, a broom, gloves, cleaning supplies, maybe a small toolkit. If you do more advanced work—like minor home repairs or furniture assembly—you can add as needed. Borrow at first if you must. Invest once you start making money.

Safety matters. Wear appropriate clothing. Lift with your legs. Bring a water bottle. Keep your phone charged. Take care of your body—it's your number one asset in this line of work.

Cleaning Hustles: Surprisingly Lucrative

Let's talk about cleaning. Many people don't realize how profitable this can be. Deep cleaning kitchens, garages, bathrooms, or even cars is hard work—but it pays.

There's a reason cleaning services thrive. People crave cleanliness, but few want to do the dirty work. You don't need a commercial license or fancy tools. Just be thorough, dependable, and respectful of people's space.

Offer packages: "Standard house cleaning – 2 hours – $60" or "Garage deep clean – $80 flat rate." Bring your own supplies and have a checklist. Clients love knowing exactly what they're paying for.

Over time, you can even specialize—offering move-out cleans for renters, post-party cleanups, or clutter-reduction services. Each niche opens a new door.

Real Stories, Real Hustle

I know a man who started out just offering to mow lawns in his neighborhood. No branding, no ads—just his feet on the pavement and a handwritten flyer. Within two months, he had regular clients, was booking $600 weeks, and eventually expanded into leaf removal, snow shoveling, and gutter cleaning. All from one decision to knock on a few doors.

Another woman I met built a steady income cleaning homes for busy moms. She offered flexible hours, customized services, and charged $25/hour. Within a few weeks, she was booked solid—and she did it with nothing more than a mop, a vacuum, and a strong work ethic.

This hustle works because it's rooted in something timeless: helping others. It's not glamorous, but it's deeply needed. And when you show up consistently, people start to rely on you. That's when things change.

Scaling Up

Once you've built a small client base, think about how to scale. Can you take on bigger jobs? Bring in a friend to help on large projects? Offer monthly service packages? Create a simple Facebook page where people can book you?

Consistency is key. Show up on time. Be polite. Clean up after yourself. Overdeliver. Every job is an audition for more work. And when your name gets passed around, your phone won't stop ringing.

Eventually, you may even formalize your hustle into a registered business—"Phoenix Home Services" or "Hustle Handyman." Offer digital payments. Make invoices. Build trust, one handshake at a time.

A Hustler's Note

You don't need to be tech-savvy to earn money. You don't need a college degree or a fat bank account. All you need is the decision to try—and the courage to ask for work.

If you're nervous, that's okay. Start small. Offer to clean a friend's garage for $30. Mow one lawn. Assemble a bookshelf. Just begin. The confidence will come.

Tell me what you're working on. I'll help you price, pitch, or scale it.

Odd jobs aren't just a hustle—they're a gateway. To income. To purpose. To independence. And it starts with a simple question: who needs help around here?

The answer, more often than not, is: everybody.

Let's get to work.

Onward to Chapter 10.

11.

Hosting a Garage Sale or Facebook Marketplace Blitz

There's something beautiful about turning the old into something new, about taking what's sitting in your closet, attic, or garage and transforming it into instant income. Hosting a garage sale—or staging a rapid-fire Facebook Marketplace blitz—is one of the simplest, quickest, and most emotionally satisfying ways to earn money overnight. You're not just decluttering your space; you're unlocking value you've already paid for, sitting silently in the shadows of your life.

This is not just about junk. It's about opportunity. Every dusty toaster, forgotten DVD box set, extra phone charger, and pair of jeans you no longer wear is a stepping stone to your next $100. Every item you no longer use can help fund your next hustle, pay for groceries, or cover rent. And it doesn't take weeks of planning. You can decide today—and sell tomorrow.

The Emotional Power of Letting Go

Let's be real—many of us hold onto things for emotional reasons. That dress you wore once. That book you swore you'd read. That chair you were going to reupholster. We become emotionally entangled with our belongings. But the truth is, clutter can keep us stuck—mentally, physically, and financially.

Hosting a garage sale is a physical and symbolic act of movement. It's you saying, "I'm ready for more." It's you deciding to trade what no longer serves you for what can. When you let go of things you don't need, you create room—not just in your house, but in your life. Room for money, room for energy, room for growth.

The 24-Hour Prep Plan

You don't need weeks of planning. All you need is a mission, some hustle, and a little bit of strategy. Start by walking through every room of your house with a laundry basket or bin. Ask yourself one question: Have I used this in the last 6 months? If not, it goes in the bin. Be ruthless. That blender that takes up counter space? That stack of old video games? That third winter coat? Sell them.

Once you've gathered a solid pile, sort items by category—clothes, electronics, kitchenware, tools, toys, books, décor. This will help you both for physical display and online posting. Give everything a quick wipe or dust to make it presentable. Take a moment to look at that pile. That's your money right there. Your rent, your groceries, your freedom—just waiting to be claimed.

Garage Sale Tactics

If you're going the traditional route, set up tables, blankets, or racks in your driveway, front yard, or garage. Use boxes for smaller items. Label everything clearly. People don't like guessing—clear pricing removes friction.

Have a money box with change—small bills and coins. Consider using a free payment app like Cash App, Venmo, or PayPal for buyers who don't carry cash.

Post signs at intersections with arrows and bold print. Keep it simple: "GARAGE SALE – 123 Main St – Sat 8am." Post in Facebook garage sale groups, Craigslist, Nextdoor, and local apps. Mention high-value items like electronics, tools, or baby gear—it draws attention.

Set up early and be ready for early birds. The first two hours are the most profitable. Greet people warmly, offer deals for bundled items, and always be open to haggling—it's part of the culture.

The Facebook Marketplace Blitz

If you don't want foot traffic or don't have the space, go digital. Facebook Marketplace is one of the most powerful tools for turning clutter into cash. It's free, local, and fast. Plus, the audience is enormous.

Take 3–5 clear photos of each item. Use natural light and different angles. Be honest about condition. Write descriptions that are simple and direct:

"Samsung microwave – works great, just upgraded – $30"
"Men's winter jacket – size L – like new – $20"

List aggressively. Post 10–20 items in a single evening. The goal is speed. Price to sell, not to haggle. Include "OBO" (or best offer) if you're flexible. Always answer messages quickly—buyers often move on fast.

Use multiple platforms: Craigslist, OfferUp, LetGo, local buy/sell groups. The more eyes on your listings, the more cash in your hand.

Bundle and Upsell

Here's a powerful trick: bundle items. Sell books in lots, clothes in bags by size, or tools as a set. It moves more items faster and makes pricing easier.

When people come to pick up one item, show them what else you have. Lay out items visually. Create a small "$5 and under" section. People rarely leave with just one thing.

Safety and Communication

If you're meeting buyers from Facebook Marketplace, always meet in a public place—gas station, parking lot, even the local police department's lot. If they're picking up from your home, keep the transaction outside and have someone with you if possible.

Be polite but firm. Don't hold items for more than a day unless you've been paid. Don't get emotionally attached—remember, the goal is to move items and make money.

Pricing Psychology

Price emotionally, not logically. What would YOU pay for it if you saw it secondhand? Start a little high to leave room for haggling, but be willing to accept less. People love a deal—and you love clearing space.

Use pricing stickers, color codes, or signs to make it easy. And have a "Free" bin for small junk—it draws people in and makes them more likely to buy.

When the Dust Settles

At the end of the day—literally—you'll have a pile of cash, a cleaner home, and a lighter heart. There's something deeply liberating about letting go. You'll sleep better knowing you've taken action, reclaimed space, and turned things you don't use into money you can spend.

And guess what? This isn't just a one-time thing. You can do a digital blitz every month. You can pick up free items on Facebook and flip them. You can help friends clean out their homes and split the profits. You've just tapped into a powerful, repeatable income stream.

I'll help you write your listings, price your stuff, or even plan your garage sale strategy.

This book you're reading? It started with hustle. With selling what I had. With turning clutter into clarity. And you can do it too.

The world doesn't need more stuff—it needs more action. And you're the one taking it.

Let's keep going. Part III is calling.

Onward to Chapter 11.

Part III: Low-Capital Side Hustles

12.

Print-on-Demand Merch

There's something incredibly powerful about seeing your ideas come to life—and even more powerful when those ideas start making you money, often while you sleep. Print-on-demand (POD) is one of the most exciting low-capital hustles you can start tonight. No inventory, no upfront printing costs, and no complicated logistics. Just your creativity, a free design tool, and a platform that handles the rest. And yes, it's real money.

In a world where originality, expression, and niche interests are currency, POD lets you tap into markets with almost no financial risk. Want to make t-shirts for cat lovers who do yoga? Done. Hoodies for introverts who love coffee and books? Go for it. Mugs with funny phrases only accountants understand? That's gold.

Why POD is a Low-Risk Goldmine

You don't need to buy 100 shirts or rent a storage unit. With platforms like Teespring, Redbubble, Printful, and Merch by Amazon, you only upload your design. When someone buys it, the platform prints, ships, and even handles customer service. You keep a cut. It's the definition of a passive hustle with active potential.

This is especially powerful if you're starting from zero. You don't need to be a designer. You can use free tools like Canva or even AI-based generators to get started. The barrier isn't skill—it's commitment. You just need to get started.

Getting Started: Tools You Need

1. Design Tool: Use Canva, Photopea, or even simple tools like Microsoft Paint for basic ideas.

2. Platform: Choose one–Redbubble and Teespring are easiest for beginners. Merch by Amazon has the biggest reach but requires an invite or application.

3. Theme/Niche: Focus is everything. Don't just design for "everyone." Design for specific audiences. Think nurses, teachers, gamers, plant moms, gym lovers, introverts. Specific wins.

Finding Your Niche

A niche is the soul of POD. You're not just selling a t-shirt–you're selling identity. Pride. Humor. Belonging. Think of the shirts you've seen with slogans like "I Paused My Game to Be Here" or "Dog Moms Are Cooler Than You." They don't just say something–they mean something to someone.

Start by brainstorming five things you're passionate about. Then explore subcultures and interests in those spaces. Go on Reddit. Join Facebook groups. Find what they talk about, what they laugh about, what inside jokes they share. Then design for them.

Designing Without Being a Designer

You don't need to be Van Gogh. You need to be clever. Words sell. Text-based designs dominate. Pair a witty slogan with clean typography and you're in business.

Sites like Canva offer free templates. You can also find free-to-use icons and graphics on places like Flaticon or Pixabay. Just be sure you have the right to use them commercially. Better safe than sorry.

The Power of Merch by Amazon

Let's talk about the big dog. Merch by Amazon is like selling t-shirts on steroids. You upload your design, pick your price, and Amazon puts it in front of millions of customers. When someone buys, they print and ship it. You earn royalties.

Pros:

Massive reach

Trusted platform

Seamless fulfillment

Cons:

Approval required

Limited slots at first

Competitive

But once you get in, the upside is huge. One well-timed design can bring you hundreds—even thousands—without touching a box or talking to a buyer.

Facebook + POD = $$$

Here's a trick: go into niche Facebook groups and observe. Find what people are passionate about. Then design a product just for them. Don't post it directly—build a simple Etsy or Redbubble listing and share it when relevant or run a $5 Facebook ad targeting that audience.

It's not just about designs. It's about connection. The closer you get to what people love, fear, laugh at, or stand for—the more you sell.

Common Mistakes to Avoid

1. Being too general – "Funny shirt" isn't a niche. "Funny nurse shirt" is.

2. Ignoring trends – Look at trending hashtags, pop culture moments, and seasonal events.

3. Low-quality images – Pixelated graphics don't sell. Use high-res.

4. Giving up too fast – This isn't a one-shot game. Test, tweak, repeat.

My First Month with POD

When I first started, I made a few coffee-themed designs on Redbubble. They were terrible. One said “But First, Espresso Yourself” in Comic Sans. I thought it was clever. It sold zero.

But I kept going. I studied bestselling shirts. I learned what people actually wanted. My next batch focused on a niche Facebook group for women who ran marathons. That month, I made $173. The month after, $479. And then it clicked.

One design that said “Running Is My Therapy” made over $1,000 in one week. Just a sentence. On a shirt. On a platform I didn’t pay to use. That’s the magic.

Let Me Help You Start

This hustle changed my life. It’s why I included it in this book. If you want help with niches, design ideas, or how to get started, email me. I’ll walk you through it:

princephoenix959@gmail.com
danieldavidphoenix@gmail.com

You don’t need a studio, a warehouse, or investors. You just need a vision, a voice, and a willingness to try. Tonight, you could upload your first design. Tomorrow, you could wake up to your first sale.

You’ve got this.

Let’s keep moving.

Onward to Chapter 13.

13.

Starting a One-Day Service Business

Turn Time and Talent Into Instant Income

You don't need a storefront, a business license, or a giant marketing plan to start making money from a service today. All you really need is a problem to solve, the willingness to help someone out, and the courage to put yourself out there. A one-day service business isn't about building an empire—at least not yet. It's about getting up in the morning and ending the day with cash in your pocket because you used your time and skills to offer something someone needed. Whether it's washing windows, assembling IKEA furniture, or organizing a messy closet, the demand for small, local services is endless. And the best part? You don't need any money to start—just hustle, confidence, and maybe a bottle of Windex.

Let's face it: not everyone has a product to sell, a car to rent out, or a brilliant design idea to slap on a T-shirt. But everyone has time. Everyone has hands. Everyone has a brain. A one-day service business taps into those universal assets. It's a reminder that you don't have to reinvent the wheel to be useful. In fact, the simpler the service, the faster you'll get hired. People are busy, overwhelmed, and in need of someone who can take a task off their plate. That someone can be you—today.

One of the most overlooked truths about making money quickly is that people will happily pay to avoid inconvenience. Think about how many people would rather pay $50 for someone to set up their TV, mount a shelf, or clean out their garage than spend a frustrating Saturday doing it themselves. You don't need to be an expert—you just need to be capable. And if you're not capable yet? There are thousands of five-minute YouTube tutorials that can make you capable in no time. The barrier to entry has never been lower. The demand has never been higher. The opportunity has never been more immediate.

So where do you start? First, take inventory of what you can do right now. Can you mow a lawn? Clean a bathroom? Move furniture? Walk dogs? Install basic tech gear? Help someone run errands? You don't need ten ideas—you need one solid service that you can deliver reliably, safely, and confidently. From there, the goal is to find your first client—fast. The quickest way is to start with people you already know: post on your personal social media, text your friends, call family members, and say, "Hey, I'm offering [this service] today and have a couple open spots. Let me know if you or anyone you know needs help!" This approach is personal, non-salesy, and often gets results within hours.

Still worried you don't have a standout skill? Don't be. Some of the most successful one-day hustles are rooted in things most people consider ordinary. For example, laundry folding. Yes—there are countless people who would gladly pay for someone to pick up, fold, and drop off their clean laundry, especially busy parents or professionals. The same goes for pantry organization, holiday decoration setup, closet cleanouts, or running simple errands. When you offer your time as a service, you tap into the one thing people value more than money—time itself.

Let's walk through a real-world example. Imagine it's 9 a.m. You decide you're going to offer a garage cleanout service for $75 flat. You post it on your Facebook page and in a local community group: "Got a cluttered garage? I'm offering same-day cleanouts—let me do the dirty work so you can enjoy your space again! $75 flat, slots open today." By 11 a.m., someone messages you. By 12:30 p.m., you're hauling boxes and sweeping floors. By 3 p.m., you've finished the job, pocketed the cash, and taken photos of the transformation to use as marketing for your next client. That's not a dream scenario—it's a repeatable process. Every single person has a "garage" in their life that needs clearing out, and if you become the person who offers to fix that, you've found your niche.

Now, let's be real. The biggest hurdle for most people isn't skills or logistics—it's fear. Fear of being rejected. Fear of looking foolish. Fear of not doing a perfect job. But perfectionism kills speed, and when you're trying to hustle overnight, speed is everything. So instead of trying to be perfect, aim to be helpful. That's it. Show up on time, communicate clearly, do the job with care, and ask for feedback or a review when you're done. That alone puts you miles ahead of anyone who's still waiting to "feel ready."

As you build momentum, you'll start seeing patterns. Maybe you notice that more people want furniture assembled than yard work done. Or that dog walking is easier to fill than running errands. Lean into what works. Create a quick name for your service, even if it's just something playful like "Fix-It Frank" or "Errands by Emma." Use Canva to make a free flyer or simple logo. Start a free business page on Facebook or Instagram to build credibility. These small touches help you look more legit, which makes people more willing to hire you—even if you're still just one person with a phone and a goal.

Another smart move? Partner with others. If you know someone who's good with tools, team up and offer two-person handyman jobs. If your neighbor is looking for side cash, co-host a Saturday errand service blitz. Working with others not only lets you divide labor—it also multiplies reach. You each bring your own network, and referrals start snowballing. Plus, it makes the work more enjoyable. Hustling doesn't have to mean hustling alone.

And don't forget to document everything. Take before-and-after photos. Ask for short testimonials. Share your stories online. The more you show your value, the more people will trust you. This is how a one-day hustle turns into a weekly gig... then a part-time income... then, if you want, a full-blown business. Some people start with a single closet organization and end up launching a personal organizing company. Others start with one yard mow and end up managing a small landscaping crew. You don't have to aim for that—but it's nice to know it's possible.

When you're starting out, pricing can feel awkward. Here's a tip: don't undersell yourself, but also don't overthink it. For most one-day services, flat-rate pricing works better than hourly. It makes it easier for customers to understand the value and easier for you to quote quickly. Want to offer dog walking? Try $15 for a 30-minute walk. Want to assemble furniture? Offer $40 for small jobs, $60 for larger ones. Cleaning out a garage? $75–$100 depending on size. Adjust as you go based on effort and time. If you consistently find yourself underpaid, raise your rates. If no one bites, offer an early discount for the first five customers to get traction.

Let's take it even deeper: how can you make this kind of hustle repeatable? The answer lies in systems. Create a basic checklist for your service. Build a simple routine for client communication: intro message, booking confirmation, follow-up message, payment request, and thank-you note. Use free apps like Google Calendar for scheduling, Square or Venmo for payments, and Canva or Instagram for marketing. With these low-effort systems, you'll cut down on time spent figuring things out and free up energy to actually serve more people.

Finally, let's talk about dignity. One of the biggest lies people believe is that service work is "beneath" them. Nothing could be further from the truth. Showing up, solving a problem, and earning honest money is never beneath anyone. It's brave. It's smart. It's the kind of work ethic that creates stories, confidence, and future opportunities. Every successful entrepreneur has a story about "that time I did X just to get by." These are the kinds of experiences that build character and cash flow.

If you're still wondering whether this hustle is for you, ask yourself one simple question: "Do I want to end today knowing I made money from nothing but my effort?" If the answer is yes, then get moving. Choose a service. Offer it boldly. Deliver it well. Let today be the day you stopped waiting and started doing. Because once you realize how much power you already have, the game changes forever.

14.

Pet Sitting, Dog Walking, or Babysitting

Turn Your Love for Pets or Kids Into Cash

If you've got a love for animals or kids, then why not turn that passion into a money-making hustle? Pet sitting, dog walking, and babysitting are some of the easiest side hustles to get into, and they can bring in a solid stream of income. The beauty of these services is that they cater to a need many people can't fulfill themselves. Pet owners and parents alike often need someone trustworthy to look after their loved ones while they're at work, traveling, or just needing a break. And lucky for you, they're willing to pay for it.

Think about it. Every day, thousands of families are scrambling for help with their pets or children. Whether it's a busy professional needing someone to walk their dog during the day or a parent looking for a reliable babysitter for a night out, there's a consistent demand for these services. Unlike many other hustles, pet sitting, dog walking, and babysitting often come with repeat customers. Once you build trust, it's easy to land recurring gigs, meaning this hustle could bring you regular, steady income.

Why Pet Sitting and Dog Walking Are So Profitable

Pet sitting and dog walking may sound like simple tasks, but they're high-demand services, especially as more people treat their pets like family members. In fact, Americans spent over $30 billion on pet services in 2023, and that number is only growing. With more people adopting pets, especially during the pandemic, the demand for these services is higher than ever. People need someone reliable to take care of their furry friends while they're away, and they're often willing to pay well for it. The best part? You don't need much to start.

Let's break it down.

Pet Sitting
Pet sitting involves looking after a pet in the owner's home. This could mean feeding, playing, providing companionship, or letting the pet out for bathroom breaks. Depending on the pet and the needs, this could range from a quick visit once a day to staying overnight with the pet. This service is perfect for people who travel frequently or work long hours. Pet owners appreciate the peace of mind that comes with having a trusted person care for their animals in their own environment.

Dog Walking
Walking dogs isn't just for fun—it's a serious business. A walk can range anywhere from 15 minutes to an hour or more, and many pet owners are willing to pay for regular dog walking sessions, especially if they work long hours or live in areas with limited outdoor spaces. Dog walking isn't just exercise for the dog; it's an opportunity for socialization, mental stimulation, and relief from boredom. And in return, you're getting paid to get some fresh air and spend time with furry friends.

Babysitting
Babysitting is another hustle that's been around for generations, but it's still incredibly profitable. Parents often need someone reliable to watch their children while they go out for a date night, attend work events, or handle other responsibilities. Babysitting can involve anything from watching TV and putting kids to bed to helping with homework or taking them to activities. If you enjoy working with children, this is a great hustle to start. It's also an excellent way to build rapport with families, which can lead to long-term gigs and referrals.

Getting Started: Quick, Simple, and Smart

The best part about these hustles is that they're easy to get started. You don't need a degree in animal behavior or early childhood education (although those would be great if you have them). You just need a love for pets or kids, reliability, and a responsible attitude.

Here's how to jumpstart your pet sitting, dog walking, or babysitting business:

1. Assess Your Skills and Interests
The first step is to figure out where your interests lie. Do you love animals? Are you comfortable taking care of kids? Are you good at following schedules and instructions? If you have any experience—whether it's volunteering at an animal shelter or taking care of younger siblings—that's a bonus. But even if you have no experience, people are often willing to hire someone who is dependable, caring, and proactive. Make sure to highlight your personality and trustworthiness when talking to potential clients.

2. Set Up an Online Presence
Even for a hustle like this, it's important to get your name out there online. Create a simple, professional profile on pet sitting and dog walking platforms like Rover or Wag. For babysitting, websites like Care.com or Sittercity can help you find local gigs. These platforms make it easier for you to get noticed by people who need your services. Having a profile with a clean, friendly photo and a solid description of your services will go a long way in building trust. If you can, get testimonials from previous clients (even if they're friends or family) to showcase your reliability.

3. Get Certified or Take a Course
While it's not necessary to have certifications to get started, taking a short course can add credibility to your service. Websites like Petco and the American Red Cross offer training programs in pet first aid or CPR for animals. For babysitting, the Red Cross also offers a babysitting course that teaches basic childcare skills and safety. Not only does this increase your

marketability, but it can also give you the confidence to handle emergency situations.

4. Start with Local Connections
If you don't have any experience, start with people you know. Ask your friends and family if they need a pet sitter or if they know someone who does. Word of mouth is incredibly powerful in this industry, especially when starting out. You can also post in local Facebook groups, neighborhood apps, and community boards to find potential clients. Let people know you're offering pet sitting or dog walking services for a limited time to build your portfolio.

5. Build a Reputation
As with any hustle, reputation is key. Always show up on time, be courteous, and go the extra mile. If you're walking a dog, make sure they get the exercise they need, and don't be afraid to send the owner updates or pictures of their pet. Parents will appreciate knowing their children are in good hands. After completing a job, ask for feedback and reviews to continue building your online presence. The more positive reviews you collect, the more likely people are to hire you.

Pricing Your Services: What You Should Charge

Pricing for pet sitting, dog walking, and babysitting will depend on your location and the level of service you're providing. That said, here are some general guidelines to help you get started:

Dog Walking: $10–$25 for a 30-minute walk. If you're walking multiple dogs, you can increase the price accordingly.

Pet Sitting: $15–$40 per visit, depending on how long you'll be with the pet and whether it's overnight. Some sitters also offer discounts for multiple visits per day or long-term arrangements.

Babysitting: $10–$25 per hour, depending on your location and the number of children. Babysitting rates can also increase if you're expected to perform additional tasks like cooking, driving, or helping with homework.

It's always a good idea to check the going rates in your area to ensure you're competitive. If you're new to the business, you might want to start with lower prices to attract clients and gradually increase your rates as you build a client base and gain more experience.

Scaling Up Your Hustle

As you begin to build a steady stream of clients, you can start to think about scaling up your hustle. One way to do this is by offering packages. For example, you could create a dog-walking subscription where clients pay a set rate for a week's worth of walks. You could also look into offering other pet-related services, like grooming or pet photography, to expand your offerings.

Another way to scale up is by leveraging referrals. Ask your clients to refer their friends and family to you in exchange for a discount on their next service. This way, you're essentially letting your satisfied customers do the marketing for you, and you're getting paid in the process.

If you find you enjoy the hustle and are getting great reviews, you might even decide to turn it into a full-fledged business by hiring others to help with pet sitting or dog walking. The possibilities are endless.

Conclusion: A Hustle That's Both Fun and Lucrative

Pet sitting, dog walking, and babysitting are some of the most accessible hustles you can start today. If you love animals or children, these services offer a way to get paid for doing something you genuinely enjoy. Plus, they come with the added bonus of creating meaningful connections with your clients—and, in some cases, their furry or little loved ones.

With minimal startup costs and flexible hours, this is a hustle that can fit into anyone's schedule, no matter what else you're doing. If you're looking for a quick and rewarding way to make money, look no further than the wonderful world of pets and kids. Whether you're taking a dog for a walk, looking after a toddler for a few hours, or giving a cat some company while their owner is away, you can earn money while doing something fulfilling.

So, what are you waiting for? The pets—and the parents—are waiting for you to show up.

15.

Car Washing or Detailing in Your Neighborhood

Turn Dirt Into Dollars with a Mobile Car Care Business

Imagine this: It's a Saturday morning, the sun is shining, and you've got a bucket of soapy water, a hose, and a few microfiber cloths. By noon, you're $100 richer, all from cleaning someone's car. It's not a dream—it's a hustle you can start right now. Car washing and detailing is one of the easiest and most profitable one-day businesses you can get into. The beauty of this hustle lies in its simplicity: people need clean cars, and they're willing to pay to have it done professionally, especially if they don't have the time, tools, or motivation to do it themselves. Best of all, you don't need a fancy location or expensive equipment to start. You can do it right in your driveway, at a customer's house, or even in a parking lot.

The demand for car washing and detailing services is constant, and it only grows when the weather gets warmer. Think about it: people are constantly using their vehicles, but few make the time to maintain them. Whether it's a mom with a minivan full of snack crumbs or a professional who wants to impress clients with a spotless ride, there's always someone looking for a little extra TLC for their car. And while there are big carwash chains, they often can't offer the same personalized touch and convenience that you can. That's where you come in.

Why Car Washing and Detailing is a Perfect Hustle

Car washing and detailing aren't just about making cars shine—they're about providing a service that people value. A clean car isn't just about looks; it's about maintaining the vehicle's condition, protecting the paint, and making it feel like new again. Detailing can involve a range of tasks, from washing and waxing to vacuuming the interior, cleaning the windows, and treating the upholstery. Some people might want a quick wash and dry, while others are willing to pay more for a deep clean and full detailing. No matter what, there's money to be made by helping people keep their cars in top condition.

This hustle is ideal for anyone looking to make money fast. It's highly repeatable and can become a source of steady income, especially as you build a client base. The best part? You can start with just a few basic supplies and expand as you gain more experience. If you enjoy working outdoors, don't mind getting your hands a little dirty, and want a hustle that can pay well for a few hours of work, car washing and detailing could be the perfect opportunity.

Getting Started: Simple Steps to Launch Your Mobile Car Care Business

Starting your car washing or detailing business doesn't have to be complicated. Here's a step-by-step guide to get you going quickly:

1. Gather Your Supplies
The first step is to collect the basic materials you'll need. While you don't need a full-scale detailing kit right away, here are the essentials:

- Car Soap and Shampoo: Opt for high-quality car soap designed to lift dirt without damaging the paint.
- Microfiber Towels: These are essential for drying and buffing the car's surface without scratching it.
- Buckets and Sponges: You'll need one bucket for soapy water and another for rinsing the sponge.

- Vacuum: For cleaning the interior of the car. A handheld vacuum or a portable wet/dry vacuum is a good start.
- Glass Cleaner: For cleaning windows and mirrors.
- Wax and Polish: To give the car's exterior a shine and protect the paint.
- Tire Cleaner and Dressing: To clean and shine the tires.
- Interior Cleaner: For vacuuming and cleaning the upholstery and dashboard.

Don't worry about buying high-end equipment just yet. You can find affordable products that get the job done without breaking the bank. Over time, as you build your business, you can upgrade your tools for greater efficiency and better results.

2. Set Your Rates

When you're starting out, you want your rates to be competitive but fair. Keep in mind that most people are looking for a reasonably priced car wash or detailing service, but they're also willing to pay more for quality. Here's a rough idea of what you could charge:

- Basic Car Wash: \$15–\$25 for a simple exterior wash, depending on the size of the car and the location.
- Interior Cleaning: \$25–\$50 for vacuuming, dusting, and wiping down surfaces.
- Full Detailing: \$75–\$150 for a complete interior and exterior clean, which may include waxing, polishing, and carpet cleaning.

If you're offering a mobile service, you can charge an additional fee for the convenience of having the service come to the client's location. You might also offer package deals, like a discounted price for regular customers or a "wash and wax" bundle.

3. Market Your Service Locally

Like many hustles, your first clients will likely come from people you know. Let your friends, family, and neighbors know that you're offering car washing and detailing services. You can also advertise in local community groups on Facebook, Instagram, or Nextdoor, where people often post about needing services. You could even post flyers around your neighborhood, offering a "first-time customer discount."

Online platforms like Craigslist and TaskRabbit also offer opportunities to advertise your service to a wider audience. The key is to get the word out and show people that you're reliable, efficient, and affordable. Share photos of your work—before-and-after shots are especially effective.

4. Provide Exceptional Service

The most important part of this hustle is delivering quality results every single time. Clients want a clean, shiny, and well-maintained car, but they also want to feel like they're getting their money's worth. Be punctual, professional, and thorough in your work. If you do a great job, clients will come back, and they'll likely recommend you to their friends and family. Word-of-mouth marketing is your best tool in this business, so always aim to exceed expectations.

In addition, you can provide extra services to make your offering even more attractive. For example, you could include tire cleaning with every car wash, or you could offer to clean the floor mats and seat covers for an additional fee. The more value you add, the more likely people are to book you again.

5. Expand as You Grow

Once you get comfortable with basic car washing and detailing, you can start to think about scaling up your hustle. Maybe you hire a helper for bigger jobs, or you invest in additional equipment like a power washer or carpet cleaner to increase the efficiency and quality of your service. You could also start offering commercial services to local businesses, like washing the cars of employees or offering fleet cleaning for small businesses with multiple vehicles.

As you build a client base and reputation, consider offering subscription services or maintenance packages. For example, a client might pay for a monthly wash or detailing at a discounted rate, giving you consistent business and steady cash flow. You can also look into collaborating with local businesses like car dealerships, rental agencies, or auto repair shops that may need a reliable car cleaning service.

Benefits of This Hustle

Car washing and detailing come with a lot of perks. For starters, it's a flexible hustle that can be done on your schedule. You can offer it part-time, or you can scale it up into a full-time business. It's a hustle that's also relatively low-cost to start—most of the materials you need can be purchased for less than $100, and you don't need a special location or storefront. All you need is a few essential tools, a mode of transportation, and the drive to get started.

Additionally, this hustle allows you to be outside and active, which can be a welcome break from desk jobs or screen time. It's a physical job, but it's also one that allows you to feel a real sense of accomplishment at the end of the day. You'll be able to see the results of your work firsthand, and you'll have happy customers who appreciate your service.

Conclusion: A Simple Hustle with Big Rewards

Car washing and detailing are classic hustles that are still as relevant and profitable today as ever. This is an accessible, low-risk way to start making money fast. It doesn't require much to get started, and it offers a wide range of potential clients, from individuals to businesses. With a little hustle, quality service, and smart marketing, you can easily turn this side job into a steady stream of income.

So, grab your cleaning supplies, start offering your services, and watch as the money rolls in. Your first few clients are just waiting for someone like you to show up and give their car the care it deserves. With the right mindset and a willingness to get your hands a little dirty, this hustle can be your gateway to consistent cash flow—and maybe even the start of your own mobile car care business.

16:

Offering Resume or Essay Services

Turn Your Writing Skills into a Money-Making Hustle

If you have a knack for writing and an eye for detail, offering resume writing or essay services could be the perfect hustle for you. There's always a steady demand for well-crafted resumes, cover letters, and essays, as people from all walks of life are looking to improve their written materials. Whether it's a college student needing help with an admissions essay, a job seeker wanting to stand out with a polished resume, or a professional looking to perfect their cover letter, you have the potential to turn your writing talent into a reliable source of income.

The beauty of this hustle is that it doesn't require a lot of upfront investment. You don't need to buy inventory or expensive tools—you simply need your computer, internet connection, and the ability to write effectively. In fact, this hustle can often be done entirely from home, allowing you to work on your own time and from the comfort of your own space. Whether you're helping someone land their dream job or ensuring that a student's essay gets the attention it deserves, your services can make a real difference in someone's life—and they're willing to pay for it.

Why Offering Resume or Essay Services is Profitable

In today's fast-paced, competitive world, everyone is looking to get an edge—whether they're applying for jobs or applying to colleges. Your ability to help people present themselves in the best possible light through their resumes, cover letters, or essays gives you a valuable service that's always in demand.

Resume Writing

A strong resume is often the key to landing an interview. However, many job seekers struggle to convey their skills and experience in a way that grabs attention. This is where you come in. Writing a compelling resume that highlights a person's achievements, skills, and qualifications in a clear and impactful way can make a world of difference. You don't need to be a professional career counselor to offer this service. If you understand the key components of an effective resume and are skilled at making it both visually appealing and content-rich, you can help clients put their best foot forward.

Cover Letter Writing

A cover letter is often just as important as the resume itself. It's the opportunity to personalize an application and explain why a candidate is the perfect fit for the job. However, writing a strong, tailored cover letter isn't easy for everyone, and many applicants struggle with this step. If you have the ability to craft persuasive and compelling cover letters, this can be a valuable service that many job seekers will gladly pay for.

Essay Services

Whether it's helping a high school student with a research paper, a college applicant with their personal statement, or a graduate student working on their thesis, the demand for essay services is high. Many students find themselves overwhelmed with assignments, struggling to meet deadlines, or unsure of how to write effectively for academic purposes. By offering essay writing, editing, and proofreading services, you can provide crucial assistance to students who need to produce high-quality academic work under tight timelines.

Getting Started: How to Launch Your Resume or Essay Service

Offering resume or essay services is relatively straightforward, especially if you have experience or a background in writing. Here's how you can quickly get started:

1. Assess Your Skills
First, think about the writing skills you possess. Are you particularly good at crafting resumes? Do you have experience writing essays for school or work? Maybe you have a knack for editing and proofreading. Whatever your strengths are, make sure to emphasize them when marketing your services. If you're offering resume services, for example, you might want to highlight any professional experience you have in a related field (like human resources or career coaching). If you're offering essay services, mention any academic writing experience or expertise you may have.

2. Set Up an Online Presence
Even if you're offering your services locally, it's essential to set up an online presence. This makes it easier for potential clients to find you, and it allows you to reach a broader audience. Consider building a simple website or setting up profiles on platforms like Upwork, Fiverr, or LinkedIn. These platforms are great for attracting clients who are actively looking for writing help. You can also join groups or forums dedicated to job hunting, education, or writing, where people may post requests for resume assistance or essay help.

3. Offer Samples and Testimonials
Potential clients want to know they can trust you to provide high-quality work. One of the best ways to showcase your skills is by offering samples of your work. If you're just starting, you might offer discounted services to friends or family in exchange for testimonials. Positive reviews and word-of-mouth referrals are powerful marketing tools in this hustle. The more people you help, the more likely you are to build a reputation and grow your clientele.

4. Set Your Rates
Determining what to charge for your services can be a bit tricky, but it's important to find a balance between affordability and the quality of your work. Research what others are charging for similar services in your area or online. Here's a general idea of what you could charge:

- Resume Writing: $50–$200, depending on the complexity of the resume and the experience of the client.
- Cover Letter Writing: $25–$75, with a custom letter tailored to the specific job.
- Essay Writing: $30–$100 per page, depending on the type of essay, research involved, and deadlines.
- Proofreading/Editing: $10–$30 per page, depending on the level of editing required.

These rates will vary based on your location, your experience, and the amount of work required, but the key is to ensure that you're offering good value while also being compensated fairly for your time.

5. Market Your Services
When it comes to marketing, you can tap into several avenues. Here are a few to get you started:

Social Media: Platforms like LinkedIn, Instagram, and Facebook are great for networking and building a following. Post helpful tips on resume writing, essay writing, or career advice to showcase your expertise and attract potential clients.

Job Boards: Websites like Craigslist, Indeed, and TaskRabbit often have sections where people post requests for resume writing or essay services. Respond to these posts promptly and professionally.

Email Marketing: If you already have a list of contacts (friends, family, former colleagues), send out an email letting them know about your services. You never know who might need help with their resume or an important essay.

6. Ensure Confidentiality and Professionalism
When offering resume or essay services, it's crucial to maintain confidentiality. Clients will trust you with sensitive personal information, such as their job history, educational background, and personal stories. Always respect this trust and keep their information private. Additionally, professionalism is key to building a successful reputation. Ensure that you meet deadlines, communicate clearly, and provide excellent customer service.

Benefits of Offering Resume or Essay Services

There are several benefits to offering resume and essay writing services. For one, it's a hustle that can be done entirely online, which means you can work from anywhere and set your own schedule. Additionally, this hustle allows you to leverage your writing skills in a way that helps others while also earning money. It's rewarding to help someone land their dream job or get into their preferred college, and that satisfaction can translate into repeat business or referrals.

Moreover, this hustle has the potential for scalability. As you gain more experience and build a reputation, you could increase your rates and take on more clients. You could also offer packages (e.g., resume + cover letter combo) or specialize in specific types of writing (e.g., executive-level resumes or admissions essays for Ivy League schools). Over time, you might find yourself with a steady stream of clients who rely on your expertise.

Conclusion: Write Your Way to Quick Cash

Offering resume or essay services is a highly accessible and lucrative hustle for those with strong writing skills. The demand for well-crafted resumes and essays is constant, and people are willing to pay for professional assistance to improve their chances of success in the job market or academia. Whether you're helping someone craft a standout resume, proofread an essay, or write a personal statement that gets noticed, you can turn your writing abilities into a profitable side hustle.

With a little effort and a solid marketing strategy, this hustle can quickly turn into a reliable income stream. Plus, it's a service that people will continue to need as long as there are job applicants, students, and individuals striving to make a good impression. So if you're ready to put your writing skills to work, it's time to start offering resume and essay services and start earning!

Part IV: Mindset & Momentum

17.

How to Scale from Hustle to Income Stream

Turning Short-Term Hustles into Long-Term Profits

You've started a hustle. You're making money, and things are moving forward—but now, the question becomes: how do you turn that one-time gig or weekend side hustle into a consistent, sustainable income stream? This is where the transition from a "hustle" to an "income stream" happens—where your side gig goes from a one-time thing to a profitable and repeatable business model. It's time to think beyond just making quick cash and start considering how to build momentum and turn your hustle into an ongoing income.

The beauty of the hustles you've already explored is that they don't require a ton of startup capital, and they can be done quickly. But in order to create something that continues to provide financial freedom, you need to move beyond "one-off" jobs and into something that can consistently generate revenue. Think about how you can grow, expand, or build systems that keep your cash flow steady without constantly having to grind for every dollar. This chapter will walk you through strategies for scaling your hustle into a reliable, income-generating venture.

1. Focus on Systems, Not Just Services

One of the key ways to scale your hustle is to shift from doing everything yourself to developing systems that can run on their own or with less direct involvement from you. Scaling is all about efficiency, and systems help you deliver your service in a more organized way. Systems free up your time and increase your capacity to take on more work.

Let's say you've started a freelance writing hustle. At first, you may be writing articles on a per-project basis, working directly with each client. But if you want to scale this hustle, you'll need to:

- Create templates or processes for writing or communication. This allows you to save time on every project, and gives clients a predictable experience.
- Automate scheduling with tools like Calendly, so clients can book time with you without the back-and-forth emails.
- Outsource tasks like editing or research to freelancers you trust, allowing you to take on more work while keeping the quality high.

If you're in a physical hustle, like car detailing, you can scale by offering packages, hiring help, or investing in more equipment that increases the efficiency of your service.

2. Build Your Client Base

As you scale, it's crucial to have a steady stream of clients. Repeat business and word-of-mouth referrals can be the key to building a sustainable income stream. To grow your client base, focus on:

- Building Relationships: Keep in touch with past clients, even after completing a job. Regular check-ins or special promotions can help keep you top of mind when they need services again.

- Offering Packages or Subscriptions: For example, if you're doing car detailing, you could offer a discounted monthly plan where clients pay a flat fee for regular washes or detailing. This turns your hustle into a recurring source of income.

- Expanding Your Services: Once you've established a base of customers, think about other services you can offer them. For example, if you're doing freelance writing, you could also offer content management or social media services.

- Always focus on delivering excellent value, and happy customers will send more business your way.

3. Invest in Tools and Resources

To scale effectively, it's often necessary to invest in tools, software, or resources that will help you do more work faster and better. This can include:

- Upgrading Equipment: If you're flipping items, you might want to invest in a storage unit, better tools, or a van to transport goods. For a mobile car-washing business, purchasing commercial-grade equipment will save you time and help you handle larger jobs.

- Investing in Software: Tools like QuickBooks for accounting, Trello for project management, or Canva for graphic design can help you streamline your processes and stay organized.

- Learning New Skills: As you grow, you may find that you need to learn new skills to keep up with your business's growth. Whether it's learning how to manage a team or mastering digital marketing, continual self-improvement can pay off in the long run.

4. Outsource and Delegate

As your hustle grows, you might find yourself overwhelmed with tasks that could be done by someone else. The key to scaling is realizing that you can't do it all alone. Whether you hire someone to assist with tasks or you use automation tools, you need to create space in your schedule to focus on growing your income stream rather than just maintaining it.

For example:

- Outsource Administrative Tasks: Hire a virtual assistant to handle scheduling, customer inquiries, or administrative work.

- Delegate Tasks to Freelancers: If you're offering a service that involves design, content creation, or research, consider hiring freelancers to help you scale.

- This frees you up to focus on the parts of your hustle that generate revenue, rather than getting bogged down by day-to-day tasks.

5. Track Your Progress and Financials

It's important to know how well your hustle is performing as you scale it. Use tracking tools to keep a close eye on your income, expenses, and overall business health. Some questions to ask yourself as you track your progress:

- What's working? Look at which services or products are most popular or which clients are returning the most. Double down on what's bringing you the most revenue.

- What's not working? If there's something in your business that's draining time or resources without yielding a solid return, it's time to reconsider your approach.

- What are your financial goals? Set clear targets for growth. Whether it's making $1,000 a month or hitting a larger target like $5,000 per month, you need clear goals to track your progress and adjust strategies as needed.

- By tracking your progress, you can ensure that your hustle isn't just a flash in the pan, but a thriving and growing income stream.

6. Automate or Digitize Your Hustle

In today's world, automation and digitization can make scaling a hustle much easier. Whether you're creating a product, offering services, or selling something, there are ways to automate repetitive tasks to save time. Some examples include:

- Setting up an online store: If you're selling a physical or digital product, you can automate your sales process with platforms like Shopify or Etsy.

- Automating Marketing: Use tools like MailChimp or Buffer to schedule and automate your email marketing and social media posts.

- Setting up Digital Products: If you're offering services like resume writing, consider creating an e-book, course, or template that clients can purchase directly from your website. This allows you to earn passive income.

- The more you can automate, the more you can scale without sacrificing time or effort.

Conclusion: Creating a Self-Sustaining Income Stream

Scaling your hustle is about more than just working harder—it's about working smarter. By setting up systems, automating where possible, and building a loyal customer base, you can transform a short-term hustle into a long-term income stream. With a little strategic planning and the right mindset, you can create a steady flow of income that grows over time.

The transition from hustle to income stream is an exciting one, but it requires effort and vision. Start small, but think big. By taking consistent steps and making the right investments, your hustle can evolve into a full-fledged business that gives you both financial freedom and a sense of accomplishment.

18:

Building a Hustler's Daily Routine

How to Stay Productive, Focused, and Consistent Every Day

One of the most powerful habits that separates successful hustlers from those who fall off track is a well-organized daily routine. If you want to consistently make money from your side hustles, you need to commit to creating and sticking to a routine that keeps you focused, productive, and moving toward your goals every single day.

While the idea of setting up a routine might sound boring or rigid, the truth is that successful hustlers rely on their routines to fuel their success. A well-structured day helps you avoid distractions, prioritize your time, and make progress—even when you feel like there aren't enough hours in the day. In this chapter, we'll explore how to build a daily routine that fits your hustle, boosts your productivity, and helps you stay on track as you chase your goals.

1. Understand Your "Why" and Your Goals

Before you jump into structuring your day, it's important to start with clarity. Why are you hustling? What do you hope to achieve with your side hustle? These answers should influence your routine, as they provide the motivation and purpose behind your daily actions. Your goals can vary—whether it's earning an extra $500 per month, turning your side hustle into a full-time business, or just achieving financial independence—but having a clear purpose will help guide you.

Once you've outlined your long-term goals, break them down into actionable daily tasks. These smaller steps will give you the momentum to move forward without feeling overwhelmed by the bigger picture. Remember, consistency is key. Even when the results aren't immediate, staying committed to your goals and making incremental progress will add up over time.

2. Prioritize Your Time

Time is your most valuable asset, especially when you're juggling a side hustle along with other responsibilities like work, family, or personal commitments. It's easy to get lost in the weeds of daily tasks and feel like you've worked hard all day without making much progress. That's why time management is crucial.

Here are a few tips for prioritizing your time effectively:

Use Time Blocks: Break your day into specific time blocks dedicated to different tasks. For example, you might block out two hours in the morning for hustling on your side business, then allocate time in the afternoon for personal errands or a full-time job. By chunking your day into blocks, you ensure that every task gets the attention it deserves.

Set Clear Priorities: Ask yourself every day, "What's the most important thing I need to accomplish today?" Whether it's responding to client emails, completing a product launch, or handling marketing tasks, prioritize the most impactful activities first. Avoid wasting time on minor tasks that can be handled later.

Eliminate Distractions: If you want to be productive, you must minimize distractions. This means silencing your phone, avoiding social media, and creating an environment where you can focus on the task at hand. Consider using apps like Forest, StayFocusd, or Freedom to block distracting websites while you work.

3. Establish Morning and Evening Routines

The best way to set the tone for a productive day is by starting and ending your day with purpose. A solid morning routine prepares you mentally for the work ahead, while an evening routine ensures you unwind and reflect on your progress.

Morning Routine:

- Start with Gratitude: Begin each day by focusing on what you're grateful for. Gratitude helps shift your mindset and sets a positive tone for the day ahead. Spend a few minutes writing down things you're thankful for or practicing mindfulness.

- Set Your Intentions: Take a few moments to plan your day. Write down your top priorities, whether it's hustling on a new project, following up with clients, or tackling a major task. This will keep you focused and intentional.

- Get Moving: Physical activity is key to boosting your energy and focus. Whether it's a short walk, yoga, or a workout, moving your body in the morning will help you feel alert and ready to take on the day.

- Eat Well: Fuel your body with a nutritious breakfast that will give you the energy to power through your hustle. Avoid sugary, processed foods that can lead to a midday slump.

Evening Routine:

- Reflect and Journal: Spend a few minutes reflecting on your day. What went well? What could you improve on? Write down your thoughts and any lessons learned to track your progress and refine your approach.

- Prepare for Tomorrow: Look ahead to the next day and get prepared. Set your goals, lay out your to-do list, and make sure you have everything ready to hit the ground running.

- Wind Down: It's important to unwind and relax before bed. Avoid checking emails or working late into the night. Instead, engage in activities that help you relax, like reading, meditation, or enjoying a cup of tea. Getting enough rest is critical to staying productive in the long run.

4. Incorporate Time for Self-Care

In the hustle culture, it's easy to get caught up in the grind and forget to take care of yourself. But without self-care, you'll quickly burn out, and your hustle will suffer. It's important to schedule regular breaks and downtime to recharge.

Take Breaks Throughout the Day: Whether it's a short walk, a 10-minute meditation session, or just stretching for a few minutes, taking breaks throughout the day can help clear your mind and boost your energy.

Invest in Your Mental Health: Side hustles can be stressful, especially when things aren't going as planned. Make sure to prioritize activities that help relieve stress and improve your mental health. Consider journaling, exercising, or talking to a friend about any challenges you're facing.

Nourish Your Body: Along with your morning routine, take time during the day to eat healthy, stay hydrated, and listen to your body's needs. Proper nutrition and exercise can improve both your mood and productivity.

5. Stay Accountable and Track Your Progress

Accountability is an essential part of building momentum and staying consistent in your hustle. The more you hold yourself accountable, the more likely you are to stick with your routine and see results.

Use a Planner or Calendar: Schedule your daily activities and keep track of your progress. You can use a physical planner or digital tools like Google Calendar or Trello to stay organized.

Track Milestones: Break your larger goals into smaller milestones, and celebrate each one as you hit it. This could be completing a certain number of sales, securing a new client, or reaching a set income goal. Recognizing your progress will keep you motivated.

Find an Accountability Partner: If possible, team up with someone who has similar goals and check in with each other regularly. Whether it's a fellow hustler, a mentor, or a friend, having someone to share your journey with can help keep you focused and motivated.

6. Adapt Your Routine as Needed

Your hustle is a dynamic process, and so should be your routine. Life happens, and sometimes things don't go as planned. Flexibility is key to staying on track.

Be Open to Change: As your hustle grows, you might find that your routine needs to be adjusted to accommodate new responsibilities or goals. Don't be afraid to tweak your schedule as necessary.

Embrace Challenges: There will be times when things don't go according to plan. Don't get discouraged. Adapt, learn, and grow from these experiences.

Conclusion: Your Routine, Your Success

Building a daily routine is one of the most effective ways to stay productive, focused, and motivated in your hustle. By setting clear priorities, creating a structured plan for each day, and taking care of your physical and mental health, you'll be in a much stronger position to succeed in the long term.

Remember, consistency is key. It's the little actions you take every day that add up to big results. By committing to your routine and making hustle a regular part of your life, you can build the foundation for lasting success and turn your side hustle into a sustainable source of income.

19.

Avoiding Scams & Burnout

Staying Sharp, Safe, and Sane in the Hustle Game

When you're out there hustling—especially on tight timelines and under financial pressure—you're more vulnerable to two major traps: getting scammed and burning out. Both can derail your momentum, kill your confidence, and drain the very resources you're working so hard to build. This chapter is about how to stay protected—mentally, emotionally, and financially—as you pursue fast, legitimate income.

Overnight hustles are exciting. There's adrenaline in the idea that you can take control of your situation and earn money within 24 hours. But not everyone who claims to offer opportunities has your best interests at heart. Scammers target people looking for fast cash, and burnout sneaks in when you're grinding nonstop without rest, strategy, or reflection. Here's how to avoid both.

1. Spotting the Scams Before They Spot You

Scams often dress up like opportunities—shiny, fast, and full of empty promises. They play on urgency, desperation, or hope, and they're often framed as "easy money" with no work required. But here's the truth: if it sounds too good to be true, it probably is.

Here are some red flags to watch out for:

- Pay-to-play gigs: If someone asks you to pay upfront to access a job, platform, or "special training," run the other way. Legitimate hustles don't require you to pay to work.

- Fake client overpayments: In freelancing or selling, scammers may "accidentally" send you too much money and then ask for a refund. Later, their original payment bounces, and you're out both the item and the refund.

- Impersonators on gig platforms: Be wary of fake job postings or shady clients on freelance platforms. Always communicate within the platform to protect yourself, and never hand over personal information (like bank logins, SSNs, or crypto wallet keys).

- Pyramid schemes disguised as "mentorship": These setups often charge high entry fees and require you to recruit others instead of selling real products or services. You're not building a hustle—you're feeding someone else's scheme.

Protect yourself by doing these three things:

- Research every opportunity or platform. Check reviews, Reddit threads, and scam watch sites.

- Use platforms with buyer protection (like Etsy, Fiverr, or eBay) when selling or freelancing.

- Trust your gut. If something feels off, don't rationalize it—walk away.

2. The Silent Killer: Hustler Burnout

Burnout doesn't happen overnight—it builds slowly, like a slow leak in a tire. You keep pushing, thinking you're being productive, but eventually the exhaustion catches up. Burnout leaves you feeling unmotivated, anxious, and even resentful of the very hustle you once loved.

Here are the early signs:

- You're constantly tired, even after sleep.
- You feel like you're always working, but not getting ahead.
- You stop enjoying the hustle—or anything else.
- You dread messages, orders, or new opportunities.

If you're here, pause. Burnout isn't a badge of honor. It's a warning sign that your hustle needs better structure, rest, or even a reset.

3. Burn Bright, Not Out: Managing Your Energy

To avoid burnout, you must treat yourself like your most valuable asset—because you are. Your creativity, energy, and drive are what make your hustle work. Protecting them is part of the job.

Here's how to hustle smart, not just hard:

- Build in recovery time: Schedule time off, even if it's just an hour a day to disconnect. You're not a machine—you need rest to perform at your best.

- Celebrate small wins: Every dollar earned, gig completed, or milestone reached deserves recognition. These moments recharge your motivation.

- Stay connected: Hustling can be isolating. Check in with friends, talk to other hustlers, or join online communities for support.

- Learn to say no: Every opportunity isn't the right one. Protect your time and energy by turning down gigs or projects that don't align with your goals or drain you more than they reward you.

4. Financial Boundaries That Keep You Safe

Financial stress is often the fuel for both scams and burnout. That's why setting boundaries around your money—how you earn, spend, and save it—is critical.

Separate your hustle money: Use a different account or digital wallet for your side income. This makes it easier to track earnings and prevents overspending.

Track everything: Use a basic spreadsheet or free app to log income and expenses. This helps you see what's working and what's wasting your time.

Invest in the hustle, not hype: Be strategic about where you put your money. Buy tools that help you grow—like better gear, website hosting, or marketing software—not empty promises or "get rich quick" systems.

5. Know When to Pivot

Sometimes, burnout isn't a matter of too much hustle—it's the wrong hustle. Not every path is meant to be scaled, and that's okay. If a hustle drains you more than it feeds you (mentally or financially), it might be time to shift.

Ask yourself:

- Is this hustle still aligned with my goals?
- Does it bring in consistent returns for the time I put in?
- Do I enjoy doing it—or is it just a means to an end?

- Give yourself permission to evolve. One of the best things about being a hustler is your flexibility. You can pivot. You can try new angles. You're not stuck.

Conclusion: Protect the Hustler, Protect the Hustle

Avoiding scams and burnout isn't just about being careful—it's about being strategic. Your time, your energy, your talent—they are currency. Spend them wisely. When you guard yourself against scams and pace yourself to avoid burnout, you don't just survive in the hustle—you thrive.

Stay sharp. Rest when needed. Question everything that promises "easy money." The real win is building something sustainable that feeds your life, not consumes it.

20.

Reinventing Yourself in 30 Days

How to Become the Hustler You Were Always Meant to Be

What if everything you thought you were—your limitations, your story, your identity—was just a starting point? What if, in just 30 days, you could begin to become the version of yourself that actually lives the hustle, not just dreams about it? This chapter isn't just about making quick cash. It's about reshaping your mindset, habits, and self-image to match the life you say you want. Reinvention doesn't take years—it takes intention, courage, and consistent action. And it starts now.

Why Reinvention Is the Real Endgame

People don't just hustle for money. They hustle for freedom. For validation. For control over their lives. But the deeper reward? Reinvention. When you start hustling, you're not just starting a side business. You're building a new identity—one that says, I create my future.

And that reinvention becomes real the moment you stop reacting to your life and start directing it.

We often underestimate how much we can change in a month. But think about it: in 30 days, you can build habits, rewire your routine, and develop a whole new level of confidence. The person you are at the end of this challenge? They might barely recognize the person who started it. That's the goal.

Week 1: Clarity & Commitment

Objective: Get crystal clear on who you want to become and what kind of hustle fits that version of you.

Journal your "why": Not just "to make money," but why now? What are you hungry for? What's at stake if you don't change?

Pick one hustle: Focus on one strategy from this book that speaks to your strengths and circumstances. One hustle. One direction. Full commitment.

Set a 30-day goal: Be specific—how much money do you want to make? How many clients, products, or sales?

Eliminate distractions: What apps, people, habits, or thoughts are keeping you stuck? Start cutting them out now.

By the end of Week 1, you should have a clear, focused vision of your hustle, your income target, and the behaviors you're replacing.

Week 2: Building the New You

Objective: Shift your habits to match the life you're building, not the one you're leaving behind.

Create a Hustler's Schedule: Wake up earlier. Work in time blocks. Build in hustle time, rest time, and learning time.

Rewire your identity: Stop saying "I'm trying to..." or "I hope to..." Start saying: "I run a business." "I provide value." "I create income."

Get uncomfortable on purpose: Make the cold pitch. Launch the product. Post your offer. Growth lives in discomfort.

Track everything: Journal daily wins, lessons, and income. You are no longer drifting. You are documenting your climb.

By the end of Week 2, you should be in motion—with habits forming, self-talk improving, and real momentum building.

Week 3: Pressure & Power

Objective: Push your limits without burning out. Learn to handle resistance like a pro.

Expect the dip: This is where doubt creeps in. You may get tired, discouraged, or distracted. That's normal. Now prove to yourself you can keep going.

Double your output: Take your hustle actions from Week 2 and increase them. More outreach. More ads. More inventory. More pitches. More effort.

Protect your energy: Get more sleep. Drink more water. Say no more often. Protect your hustle time like your life depends on it.

Celebrate mid-point progress: Whether you've made $10 or $500, you're not who you were when you started. That deserves recognition.

By the end of Week 3, you've survived the messy middle—and you're stronger for it.

Week 4: The Breakthrough

Objective: Cement your transformation—and set your eyes on what's next.

Reflect on the gains: Who are you now compared to 3 weeks ago? Write it out. Own it. You've changed. Let that be your new baseline.

Create your next 90-day plan: What happens after Day 30? Where can you scale? What's worth repeating? What's worth dropping?

Automate and delegate: What can be streamlined or outsourced? You're no longer just hustling—you're building.

Share your story: Post your journey. Tell your friends. Write it down. When you show up publicly as your new self, you make the change permanent.

By the end of Week 4, you've gone from side hustler to full-blown reinvention mode.

This Isn't Just a Challenge—It's a Rebirth

Reinventing yourself isn't about pretending to be someone else. It's about finally becoming the version of you that's been buried under fear, fatigue, and excuses. This is about reclaiming your power. About recognizing that you don't need permission to shift your life. You need decision. Repetition. Belief.

So here's the 30-day truth:

You can make real money.

You can break toxic patterns.

You can build momentum fast.

You can stop being stuck.

You can start being you, unapologetically and on your own terms.

30 Days. That's all it takes to change everything.

You don't need a new year. You don't need a miracle. You need a plan, a hustle, and a promise to yourself that you won't quit—because the next version of you is already waiting.

21.

The 24-Hour Hustle Plan

Make Money by This Time Tomorrow

You've read the strategies. You've seen the examples. You've built a mindset that knows how to spot opportunity and take action. Now it's time to move. This chapter is your no-excuses, minute-by-minute game plan for making real money within 24 hours—starting right now.

This isn't theory. This is application. If you woke up today with zero in your account and needed cash by tomorrow, what would you actually do? This plan is for that moment. Whether you're starting from scratch, looking for a fast win, or testing the waters, this 24-hour hustle plan will help you act fast, stay focused, and earn.

Phase 1: The First Hour — Choose and Commit

Set a timer. You don't get to think about it all day—you choose your hustle now.

1. Pick one hustle from this book that fits your skill set and current access. Think:

- Do you have something you can sell?
- Can you offer a service today?
- Can you deliver, clean, write, walk, flip, or rent?

2. Pick your platform or strategy:

- Selling something? List it on Facebook Marketplace, eBay, or OfferUp.
- Offering a service? Post on local groups, Nextdoor, Fiverr, or TaskRabbit.
- Delivering? Sign up immediately for DoorDash, Uber Eats, or Instacart.
- Tutoring or freelancing? Get on Upwork, Craigslist Gigs, or reach out to friends.

3. Commit to one goal: "I will make $X by [insert time]." Don't aim for perfection. Aim for money in motion.

Phase 2: Hours 2–5 — Create the Offer and Go Live

Now that you've picked your path, get your first version out. Fast.

1. Take photos or write a short, clear offer:

- "Available today: I'll mow your lawn for $25."
- "Selling this Bluetooth speaker—great condition, $40 OBO."
- "Need a resume polished fast? I'll do it today for $30."

2. Post it everywhere relevant:

- Use Facebook groups, Instagram Stories, Twitter, Craigslist, Fiverr, etc.
- Send personal messages to people who might need what you offer. (Yes, slide into DMs—politely.)

3. Include urgency and availability:

- "Available today only."
- "First come, first served."
- "Can deliver within an hour."

Don't wait. Don't polish forever. You're not building a brand—you're making money now.

Phase 3: Hours 6–12 — Hustle, Deliver, and Follow Up

You should now have leads or some interest. This is your grind window.

1. Respond fast. If someone messages you, answer immediately. Delay kills momentum.

2. Overdeliver. Do what you said you would—and do it well. People remember service that exceeds expectations.

3. Ask for referrals or repeat business:

"Thanks again! If you know anyone else who needs this, feel free to share."

"Happy to offer another round at a discount if you need more help."

Even if you only get one customer today, turn that one into two. This is how hustlers think.

Phase 4: Hours 13–18 — Multiply the Motion

You've got something moving. Now it's time to squeeze the most out of it.

1. Duplicate the listing in multiple buy/sell groups or gig apps.

2. Batch your effort: If you're walking dogs, schedule multiple in the same time slot. If you're doing resume services, offer a same-day turnaround premium.

3. Stack your day: Can you flip something and do food delivery? Can you offer a service while waiting for buyers?

Money likes movement. The more you do, the more gravity you build.

Phase 5: Hours 19–24 — Reflect, Cash Out, and Reinforce

The hustle doesn't end when you get paid. It ends when you reflect and lock in the lesson.

1. Withdraw or count your cash. Whether it's $40 or $400, you did that.

2. Ask yourself:

What worked today?

What was harder than expected?

What would I do differently tomorrow?

3. Decide what's next:

Will you repeat this hustle tomorrow?

Will you build on it and turn it into a system?

Will you explore a new angle using this momentum?

Your First $50 (or $500) Is a Signal

This is more than just one day's work. It's proof that you are capable. That the ideas in this book work. That fast money doesn't have to be shady, desperate, or random—it can be intentional, strategic, and empowering.

Let this 24-hour plan be your emergency button, your reset switch, your momentum kickstarter. Anytime you feel lost, broke, or stuck—pull it out. You know what to do. You know how to move.

You're not just a reader anymore. You're a hustler.

Next stop: The Conclusion – Take Action Tonight. Ready to wrap this journey up and launch the reader into action?

Conclusion

Take Action Tonight

Your First $100 is Just the Beginning

Congratulations! You've made it through the full blueprint. You've read the strategies, learned the tools, and gathered the knowledge to start hustling. But here's the truth: knowledge without action is just wasted potential. The real power comes in what you do next. If you've learned one thing from this book, it should be this: You can start making money tonight—and the first $100 is just the beginning.

The Power of Starting Now

The hardest part of any hustle isn't the work—it's getting started. You've got the plan. You've got the tools. Now all that's left is to take action.

What separates those who succeed from those who stay stuck is the willingness to start, even when the path ahead isn't fully clear. If you're waiting for the "perfect moment" or the "right idea," you'll miss out on the growth that comes from jumping in with both feet. There's no such thing as a perfect hustle. There's only the hustle that's in front of you—today.

So, take action tonight. Whether you're flipping something from home, driving for DoorDash, or offering a service you know people need—just do something. The sooner you start, the sooner you'll begin building momentum, cash flow, and confidence. And that's where the magic happens.

The Next Step: Build Momentum

The first $100 you earn will feel like a victory, but it's the beginning of something much bigger. This isn't just about making quick cash—it's about turning that cash into an income stream, building systems, and scaling your hustle.

Set your next goal: Can you make $200 by the end of the week? $500 by the end of the month?

Leverage your earnings: Use your first profits to reinvest in your hustle. Buy better tools. Upgrade your skills. Automate what you can.

Grow your network: The more people you know, the more opportunities open up. Ask for referrals, network in online communities, and stay visible.

Momentum builds with every step you take. Even if that first step is small, it creates movement, and movement creates more movement. Before you know it, your side hustle will feel less like a "hustle" and more like a legitimate business.

Keep Evolving

The road ahead isn't a straight line. There will be setbacks, pivots, and moments of doubt. But if you stay flexible, stay consistent, and stay in motion, you'll build something meaningful.

Don't be afraid to evolve: Your first hustle might not be your final hustle. As you learn more and experience different opportunities, your path will likely shift. And that's great. Reinvention is part of the hustle journey.

Embrace failure as feedback: Not every idea will work. Not every gig will pay. But every setback teaches you something important. Learn from your mistakes, adapt, and keep pushing forward.

Keep pushing past comfort: The real growth happens when you push yourself outside of your comfort zone. Take bigger risks. Scale faster. Seek out the challenges that will teach you the most.

You Are the Creator of Your Future

When you take action—no matter how small—the universe responds. Opportunities open up. Confidence builds. And eventually, you'll look up and realize: you've created something from nothing. You've turned your hustle into a real income stream, and it all started because you took action tonight.

The power is in your hands. You have the skills. You have the drive. Now, it's time to get to work.

Your First $100 Is Just the Beginning

Remember, the first $100 is just the start. As you keep learning, hustling, and scaling, you'll look back at that first win as a moment that unlocked a new life for you. Your next steps are yours to take, but the one thing you can't afford to do is wait. Because every hour you wait is another opportunity lost.

So, what are you waiting for? Start hustling. Start building. And watch as your first $100 grows into something much bigger.

The hustle begins now.

Thank you for reading "Overnight Hustles: Quick Ways to Start Making Money by Tomorrow." Now go take action, and create the life you've always wanted.

Bonus Resources

As promised, here's your final gift—some tools and templates to keep you on track. These resources will help you stay organized, motivated, and ready for anything:

Bonus Resources

As you continue on your hustle journey, having the right tools and systems in place can make a massive difference. These bonus resources are designed to help you stay organized, optimize your efforts, and keep you motivated as you scale your hustle into a thriving income stream.

1. Hustle Tracker Templates

Tracking your progress is one of the most powerful ways to stay focused and measure your success. Here are templates to help you stay on top of your hustle, whether you're tracking daily sales, project milestones, or client outreach.

Template 1: Daily Hustle Tracker

Date

Hustle Activity (e.g., Flipping Items, Freelancing Gig, Delivery)

Time Spent

Money Earned

Client/Customer Feedback

Lessons Learned/Improvements

Action Items for Tomorrow

Template 2: Weekly Income Tracker

Week Ending

Total Hours Worked

Total Money Made

Expenses (Tools, ads, platform fees)

Net Earnings

New Clients/Projects

Growth Opportunities Identified

Template 3: Lead Generation & Follow-up Tracker

Lead Source (Where did the lead come from—social media, word of mouth, etc.)

Lead Status (New, Contacted, Negotiating, Closed)

Date of First Contact

Follow-up Date

Conversion Status (Yes/No)

Notes (Any special information about the lead)

Having these templates will allow you to track your hours, money, progress, and clients systematically, ensuring you don't miss any opportunity to grow.

2. Top Tools & Platforms

Using the right tools can save you time, increase your efficiency, and scale your hustle faster. Here's a list of essential tools and platforms across different types of hustles.

For Freelancers and Service Providers:

Upwork – A global marketplace for freelancers across industries.

Fiverr – Perfect for offering services like writing, graphic design, programming, and more.

Trello or Asana – Organize tasks, manage client projects, and collaborate with teams.

Calendly – Set up meetings, calls, and appointments easily with clients.

For Selling Physical or Digital Products:

eBay / Facebook Marketplace / Craigslist – Popular platforms to list second-hand or used items.

Etsy – If you're selling handmade products or digital downloads, Etsy is an excellent marketplace.

Shopify – Great for setting up your own online store for dropshipping or print-on-demand services.

Printful / Printify – Integrates with Shopify for print-on-demand merchandise like t-shirts, mugs, and posters.

Canva – Create professional designs for your products, social media, and ads, even with no graphic design experience.

For Delivery and Gig Work:

DoorDash / Uber Eats / Postmates – Delivery platforms that let you make money fast with flexible hours.

Instacart – Shop and deliver groceries, with potential to earn big in busy areas.

TaskRabbit – For finding odd jobs like furniture assembly, moving assistance, and home repairs.

For Social Media and Marketing:

Buffer / Hootsuite – Social media scheduling and analytics tools that help you manage multiple platforms from one dashboard.

Google Ads / Facebook Ads – Run ads to promote your hustle, products, or services for targeted traffic.

Mailchimp – For email marketing, collecting leads, and sending out updates or promotional emails.

For Personal Finance & Tracking:

QuickBooks – Track your expenses, invoicing, and taxes.

PayPal / Venmo / Cash App – Payment platforms that make it easy to receive money from clients or customers.

Wave – Free accounting software to manage your business finances.

3. Scripts, Ads, and Promo Tips

To stand out in a crowded market, crafting compelling ads and outreach scripts is essential. These can be used for social media posts, email outreach, and paid ads to maximize your hustle's visibility.

Social Media Post Templates:

For Offering a Service:

"Need help with [X]? I can assist! I'm offering [service] at a discounted price today only. DM me for more details!"

"Is your [insert common problem] holding you back? I'm offering fast and affordable [service]. Limited spots available, so contact me now!"

For Selling Products:

"I'm cleaning out my closet! Everything must go. Check out my latest listing—[item]. Great condition, affordable price. First come, first served!"

"Looking for a unique gift or something cool for yourself? Check out my shop! Custom-made [item]—made with love and shipped fast."

Cold Email Script for Offering Services:

Subject Line: "Helping You Solve [Problem] – Let's Chat"

Body:
Hi [Name],

I noticed that your business [or personal profile] could benefit from [specific service you offer]. I help people like you [insert benefits] and would love to offer you a quick solution.

Here's what I can do for you:

[Bullet-point benefit 1]

[Bullet-point benefit 2]

[Bullet-point benefit 3]

If you're interested, let's set up a quick 15-minute call. I look forward to hearing from you!

Best regards,
[Your Name]
[Your Contact Info]

Ad Copy for Paid Ads:

Facebook Ad for a Service:

“Tired of dealing with [problem]? We’ve got a solution for you. For a limited time, get [discount or offer] on our [service]. Message us now to claim your spot!”

Instagram Story Ad for a Product:

“Get your hands on our latest [product]—available now at a special price. Only a few left in stock, so act fast! Swipe up to shop!”

Promo Tips:

Leverage urgency: Use phrases like "Limited time only," "First come, first served," or "Only X spots available."

Show social proof: Use testimonials, reviews, or user-generated content to back up your offers.

Offer bonuses: Sweeten the deal by adding something free with a purchase or discount.

With these resources, you're now fully equipped to hit the ground running, stay organized, and promote your hustle effectively. These tools will save you time, help you scale faster, and give you the clarity to turn your hustle into a serious income stream.

Ready to dive in and start hustling? The world is waiting for you to make your move!

www.ingramcontent.com/pod-product-compliance
Lightning Source LLC
LaVergne TN
LVHW101616210926
848480LV00009B/555

* 9 7 9 8 3 4 9 3 2 1 6 7 2 *